Taschen's New York

Hotels, Restaurants & Shops

Photos Paul Ober
Texts Daisann McLane

TASCHEN's NEW YORK
Hotels, Restaurants & Shops

Angelika Taschen

TASCHEN

Hotels

Price categories without VAT:
$ up to 150 $
$$ up to 250 $
$$$ up to 450 $
$$$$ over 450 $

Preiskategorien ohne Steuern:
$ bis 150 $
$$ bis 250 $
$$$ bis 450 $
$$$$ über 450 $

Catégorie de prix, sans taxes :
$ jusqu'à 150 $
$$ jusqu'à 250 $
$$$ jusqu'à 450 $
$$$$ plus de 450 $

Restaurants

Shops

Preface | Vorwort | Préface

When I first visited New York in the early 1980s, SoHo was still a dark, non-commercial district with galleries that had just opened and innumerable artists whom almost nobody knew. Today SoHo is more and more like a shopping mall – though one with extremely interesting stores. The art scene moved on to Chelsea, but the prices there have shot up sky-high, so everything is now going over to Lower East Side. The concept of things staying the way they are is unknown in New York.

Despite – or perhaps because of – the murderous attacks on the World Trade Center in 2001 and the meltdown on Wall Street in 2008, New York is still the world's most fascinating metropolis. The reasons for this are paradoxical: although the city keeps reinventing itself, it has an oddly nostalgic atmosphere that is an irresistible magnet for almost everyone.

Nowhere else on our planet is there such a cultural mix from all corners of the world and a comparable energy ("I wanna wake up in a city that doesn't sleep", as Frank Sinatra sang). The downside for visitors, however, is being overwhelmed by a flood of galleries, restaurants, shops and hotels. And as they are constantly changing, it takes months – or actually years – to find out for yourself what you like best (this book, too, is indebted to my New York friends for some crucial tips). As hardly anyone has time for lengthy research, this book presents my selection of the many facets of New York, the result of many trips. It takes into account not so much the short-term trends and hypes, but the

Bei meinen ersten Besuchen New Yorks, Anfang der 1980er Jahre, war SoHo noch ein düsteres, unkommerzielles Viertel mit gerade eröffneten Galerien und unzähligen Künstlern, die kaum einer kannte.

Heute ähnelt SoHo immer mehr einer Shopping Mall – wenn auch einer mit höchst interessanten Läden. Die Kunstszene ist nach Chelsea weiter gezogen, wo die Preise aber so astronomisch in die Höhe geschossen sind, dass nun alles auf dem Weg in die Lower East Side ist. Stillstand ist in New York ein unbekanntes Phänomen.

Trotz – oder vielleicht gerade wegen – der mörderischen Anschläge auf das World Trade Center in 2001 und der Kernschmelze der Wall Street in 2008 ist New York immer noch die faszinierendste Metropole der Welt. Der Grund ist paradox: Obwohl sich die Stadt dauernd neu erfindet, verströmt sie ein seltsam nostalgisches Flair, dessen Anziehungskraft sich kaum jemand entziehen kann.

Den Kulturmix aus allen Winkeln der Welt und eine vergleichbare Energie („I wanna wake up in a city, that doesn't sleep", sang Frank Sinatra) findet man nirgendwo sonst auf diesem Planeten. Der Nachteil für den Besucher ist allerdings die unübersehbare Flut von Galerien, Restaurants, Läden und Hotels. Da das Angebot zudem ständig wechselt, bräuchte man Monate, eigentlich Jahre, um alleine herauszufinden, was einem am besten gefällt (auch dieses Buch verdankt einige entscheidende Tipps meinen New Yorker Freunden). Da kaum einer von uns Zeit hat für langwierige Recherchen, zeigt dieses Buch meine auf

Voilà bien trente ans que je connais New York. Je revois SoHo lors de mes premières visites : un quartier sombre, sans commerces, avec des galeries qui venaient d'ouvrir et d'innombrables artistes pratiquement inconnus. Aujourd'hui SoHo ressemble de plus en plus à un centre commercial, mais les magasins y sont très intéressants. Les artistes sont partis s'installer plus loin, à Chelsea, et les prix sont devenus si faramineux que tout le monde est maintenant en route vers la Lower East Side. On bouge à New York, ici l'immobilité est un phénomène inconnu.

New York est restée la métropole la plus fascinante du monde, en dépit – ou peut-être à cause – des attentats meurtriers contre le World Trade Center en 2001 et de l'effondrement de Wall Street en 2008. Les raisons en sont paradoxales : bien que la ville s'invente en permanence, il émane d'elle une ambiance nostalgique à laquelle il est difficile de se soustraire. « I wanna wake up in a city, that doesn't sleep », chantait Frank Sinatra : on ne trouve nulle part ailleurs un pot-pourri culturel et une énergie comparables. Revers de la médaille : le visiteur est confronté à un flot ininterrompu de galeries, de restaurants, de boutiques et d'hôtels. Et puis, la ville étant en perpétuel changement, il faudrait des mois ou plutôt des années pour trouver tout seul ce qui nous plaît le mieux (le présent ouvrage doit d'ailleurs aussi de précieux tuyaux à mes amis new-yorkais). Rares étant ceux qui ont le temps d'entreprendre de telles recherches, je présente ici une sélection, faite au cours de

classic addresses and places that have the potential to become tomorrow's classics. Personally speaking, if I eat spaghetti with truffles, then preferably in Piedmont in October and not in Cairo in December. That is why, for me, a visit to Manhattan involves eating a burger, a New York sirloin steak, a pastrami sandwich or a big slice of New York cheesecake. However, because going to McDonalds or Starbucks is a depressing experience for the taste buds and the eye, visitors should know where the best food in the most attractive and historic atmosphere is to be found: a burger at Shake Shack in Madison Square Park, a steak at Keens, a pastrami sandwich at Katz Delicatessen, a New York cheesecake at Eileen's, a martini in Bemelmans Bar and coffee at Joe.

What is extremely difficult is to make wholehearted recommendations for hotels. You might think that a city that gets 44 millions of tourists every year would have dozens of recommendable places to stay, but believe me, after trying them out for years I can only recommend very, very few with a clear conscience. Never mind! Who goes to New York to catch up on their sleep?

Have a great trip

Angelika Taschen

---

zahlreichen Reisen entstandene Auswahl der vielen Facetten New Yorks. Berücksichtigt werden nicht so sehr kurzlebige Trends und Hypes, sondern Klassiker und solche Adressen, die das Potenzial zum Klassiker von morgen haben. Ich persönlich esse zum Beispiel ungern Spaghetti mit Trüffeln im Dezember in Kairo, sondern lieber im Oktober im Piemont. Deshalb gehört es für mich zu einem Manhattan-Besuch dazu, einen Burger zu essen, ein New York Sirloin Steak, ein Pastrami-Sandwich oder ein großes Stück New York Cheesecake. Da aber ein Besuch bei McDonalds oder Starbucks ein die Zunge und Augen deprimierendes Erlebnis ist, sollte man wissen, wo es das beste Angebot in der schönsten und geschichtsträchtigsten Atmosphäre gibt: einen Burger bei Shake Shack im Madison Square Park, ein Steak bei Keens, ein Pastrami-Sandwich bei Katz Delicatessen, einen New York Cheesecake bei Eileen's, einen Martini in der Bemelmans Bar und Kaffee bei Joe.

Höchst schwierig ist es, mit Überzeugung gute Hotels zu empfehlen. Man könnte denken, dass eine Stadt mit 44 Millionen Touristen im Jahr Dutzende empfehlenswerte Unterkünfte besitzt, aber glauben Sie mir, auch nach jahrelangem Herumprobieren kann ich nur ganz, ganz wenige mit gutem Gewissen weiterempfehlen. Doch was soll's, denn wer fährt schon nach New York, um sich mal so richtig auszuschlafen?

Have a great trip

---

nombreux voyages, des multiples facettes de New York.

Les tendances éphémères et les hypes ont été délaissés au profit des classiques et des valeurs sûres qui sont les classiques de demain. Aimant mieux pour ma part manger des spaghettis aux truffes en octobre au Piémont qu'en décembre au Caire, j'avoue préférer aussi, lorsque je suis à Manhattan, manger un burger, un New York sirloin steak, un sandwich au pastrami ou un gros morceau de New York cheesecake. Néanmoins, une visite chez McDonalds ou Starbucks étant aussi affligeante pour les papilles que pour les yeux, il faut savoir où trouver ce qu'il y a de meilleur dans l'endroit le plus beau et ayant une atmosphère chargée d'histoire. C'est pourquoi je propose de manger un burger chez Shake Shack à Madison Square Park, un steak chez Keens, un sandwich au pastrami chez Katz Delicatessen, un New York Cheesecake chez Eileen's et de déguster un Martini au Bemelmans Bar et un café chez Joe.

En revanche, pour ce qui est des hôtels, il est extrêmement difficile d'en recommander un chaudement. On s'imagine qu'une ville accueillant des 44 millions de touristes chaque année possède des dizaines d'hébergements recommandables mais, croyez-moi, après avoir tenté ma chance pendant des années je n'en connais que très, très peu que je pourrais nommer sans avoir mauvaise conscience. Mais bon… qui va à New York pour dormir tout son soûl ?

Have a great trip

FOUR
SEASONS
Hotel New Yor[k]

HOTEL

HOTEL

HOTEL

HOTEL

HOTEL

HOTEL

The Bowery Hotel

Hotels

N >

West Village

The Maritime Hotel

Tribeca

The Greenwich Hotel

Hudson River Park

The SoHo Grand Hotel

60 Thompson

The Mercer

SoHo

Lafayette House

Nolita

East Village

The Bowery Hotel

Lower East Side

Brooklyn Brg

Manhattan Brg

Williamsburg Brg

Tompkins Square Park

Seward Park

Corlears Hook Park

Hamilton Fish Park

East River Park

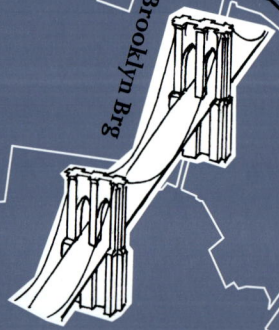

Governor Nelson A Rockefeller Park

North Cove

Esplanade

South Cove

Robert F Wagner Jr Park

Battery Pl

State St

N End Ave

Vesey St

Murray St

Warren St

Chambers St

Church St

Greenwich St

Franklin St

Leonard St

White St

Walker St

Canal St

Hudson St

Varick St

Clarkson St

Morton St

Christopher St

7th Ave S

W 4th St

Waverly Place

Bank St

Perry St

W 11th St

Washington St

W 12th St

6th Ave

W 3rd St

6th Ave

Washington Square Park

W 13th St

W 14th St

Union Sq Park

Irving Pl

E 14th St

3rd Ave

2nd Ave

Stuyvesant Square

Thompson St

W Broadway

Broadway

Mercer St

Lafayette St

Bleecker St

Crosby St

Prince St

Spring St

Kenmare St

Mulberry St

Mott St

Bowery

Chrystie St

Eldridge St

Allen St

Ludlow St

Essex St

Broome St

Grand St

Stanton St

Rivington St

Clinton St

E Houston St

Avenue A

Avenue B

Avenue C

Avenue D

E 1st St

E 2nd St

E 3rd St

E 4th St

E 5th St

E 6th St

E 7th St

E 8th St

E 9th St

E 10th St

E 11th St

E 12th St

E 13th St

E 15th St

Howard St

Greene St

Lafayette St

Centre St

Baxter St

Worth St

Park Row

Thomas Paine Park

City Hall Park

Franklin D Roosevelt Dr

Catherine St

Madison St

Cherry St

E River Piers

E Broadway

Henry St

Delancey St S

Frankfort St

Ann St

Pearl St

William St

Nassau St

Pearl St

Front St

South St

Trinity Pl

Albany St

Liberty St

Duane St

W Broadway

Beach St

N Moore St

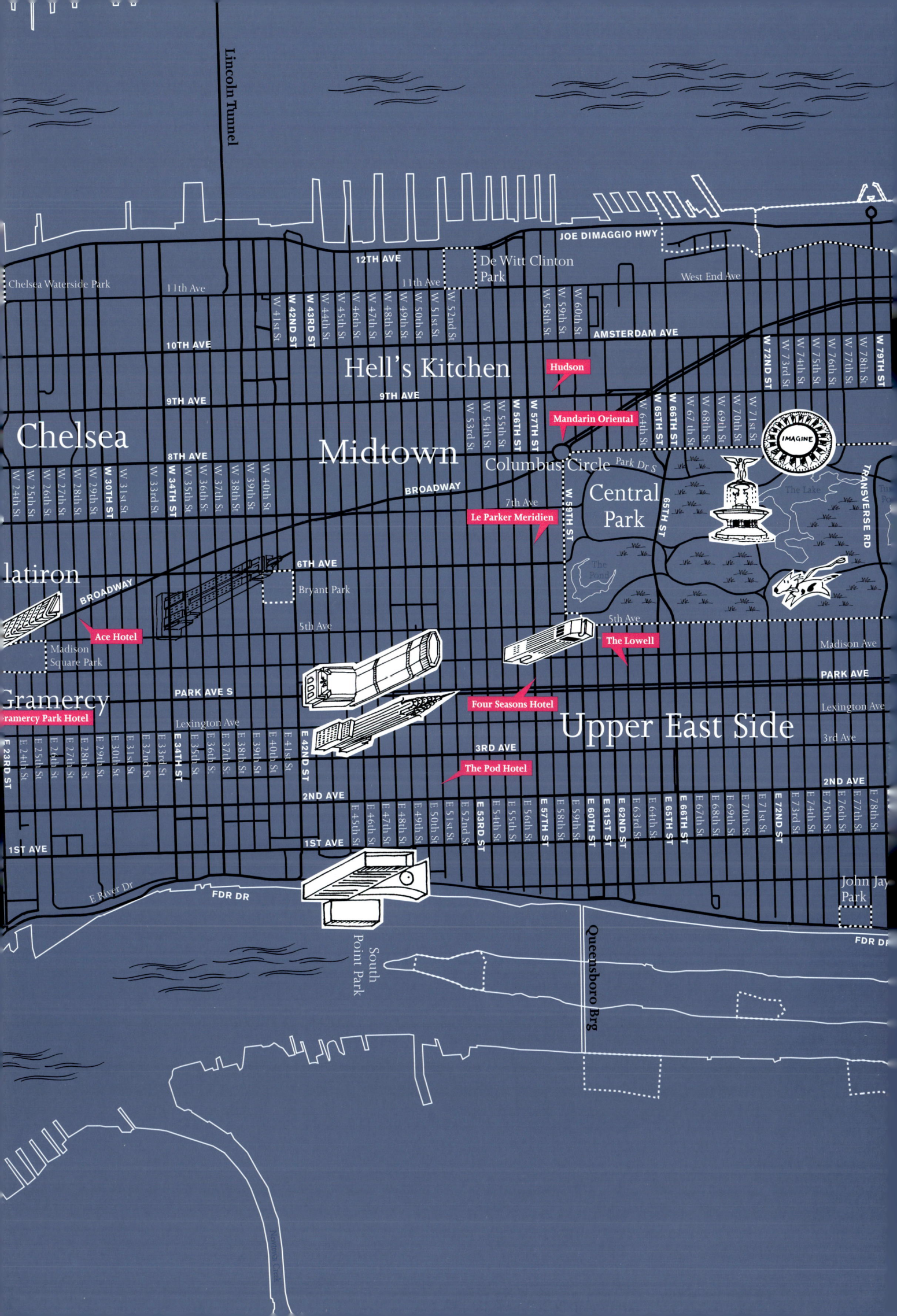

Lincoln Tunnel

JOE DIMAGGIO HWY

De Witt Clinton Park

12TH AVE

11th Ave

11th Ave

West End Ave

Chelsea Waterside Park

W 52nd St
W 51st St
W 50th St
W 49th St
W 48th St
W 47th St
W 46th St
W 45th St
W 44th St
W 43RD ST
W 42ND ST
W 41st St

W 58th St
W 59th St
W 60th St

W 72ND ST
W 73rd St
W 74th St
W 75th St
W 76th St
W 77th St
W 78th St
W 79TH ST

10TH AVE

AMSTERDAM AVE

Hell's Kitchen

Hudson

9TH AVE

9TH AVE

W 53rd St
W 54th St
W 55th St
W 56TH ST
W 57TH ST

W 64th St
W 65TH ST
W 66TH ST
W 67 th St
W 68th St
W 69th St
W 70th St
W 71st St

Mandarin Oriental

Chelsea

8TH AVE

W 30TH ST
W 31st St
W 33rd St
W 34TH ST
W 35th St
W 36th St
W 37th St
W 38th St
W 39th St
W 40th St

Midtown

Columbus Circle

Park Dr. S

Central Park

65TH ST

IMAGINE

The Lake

TRANSVERSE RD

BROADWAY

7th Ave

W 59TH ST

W 24th St
W 25th St
W 26th St
W 27th St
W 28th St
W 29th St

Le Parker Meridien

The Pond

latiron

6TH AVE

BROADWAY

Bryant Park

5th Ave

5th Ave

Ace Hotel

Madison Square Park

The Lowell

Madison Ave

Gramercy

PARK AVE S

Four Seasons Hotel

PARK AVE

Gramercy Park Hotel

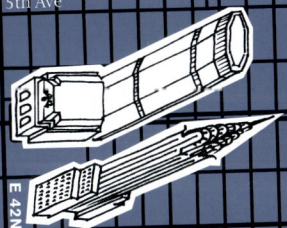

Lexington Ave

E 23RD ST
E 24th St
E 25th St
E 26th St
E 27th St
E 28th St
E 29th St
E 30th St
E 31st St
E 32nd St
E 34TH ST
E 33rd St
E 35th St
E 36th St
E 37th St
E 38th St
E 39th St
E 40th St
E 41st St
E 42ND ST

Upper East Side

Lexington Ave

3rd Ave

3RD AVE

The Pod Hotel

2ND AVE

2ND AVE

E 78th St
E 77th St
E 76th St
E 75th St
E 73rd St
E 72ND ST
E 71st St
E 70th St
E 69th St
E 68th St
E 67th St
E 66TH ST
E 65TH ST
E 64th St
E 63rd St
E 62ND ST
E 61ST ST
E 60TH ST
E 59th St
E 58th St
E 57TH ST
E 56th St
E 55th St
E 53RD ST
E 52nd St
E 51st St
E 50th St
E 49th St
E 48th St
E 47th St
E 46th St
E 45th St

1ST AVE

1ST AVE

E River Dr

FDR DR

South Point Park

Queensboro Brg

John Jay Park

FDR DR

The Mercer

147 Mercer Street, New York, NY 10012
☎ +1 212 966 6060   📠 +1 212 965 3838
reservations@mercerhotel.com
www.mercerhotel.com

Subway: Prince Street (N, R, W),
Broadway-Lafayette Street (B, D, F, V), Spring Street (6)

The Mercer may be the perfect small New York hotel. The building is beautiful – the ornate and elegant brick structure, built in 1890, was designed by William Schickel, architect of several ecclesiastical buildings in New York. It has history – originally, this was an office building for one of New York's most prominent families, the Astors. And it has an enviable location, straddling an intersection in SoHo's heart. The Mercer manages the trick of being breathtakingly stylish and reassuringly homey at the same time. Hotelier André Balazs (also owner of L.A.'s Chateau Marmont among others) and French designer Christian Liaigre have created a soothing, modernist interior, a perfect backdrop for the fascinating people who pass through. The lobby is one of New York's most celebrated hangouts, a living room where you can curl up by yourself in a corner with a coffee, or party with friends until 2am. The Mercer's attentive staff can arrange anything – and they'll even pack your bags when it's time for you to return to the less-than-perfect world.

Price category: $$$$.
Rooms: 75 luxury guest rooms including 4 suites and 2 lofts.
Restaurants: The Mercer Kitchen, contemporary food by Jean-Georges Vongerichten, breakfast, lunch, dinner. **The Lobby,** open 24 hours. **subMercer,** basement bar, open Wed–Sat (11pm–4am).
History: The six-story, Romanesque Revival building dates from 1890 and was converted to a hotel in 1998.
X-Factor: Yummy, super-luxe bathrooms are around 300 square feet – larger than most New York hotel rooms. They have oversized marble bathtubs that fit two – or more – people.

Das Mercer ist der Inbegriff eines kleinen New Yorker Hotels. Der elegante, kunstvoll verzierte Ziegelbau wurde 1890 von William Schickel entworfen, der als Architekt verschiedene New Yorker Kirchenbauten realisierte. Das einst als Bürogebäude für die berühmte New Yorker Familie Astor erbaute Hotel liegt mitten im Herzen von SoHo – und damit in beneidenswerter Lage. Dem Mercer gelingt der Spagat zwischen atemberaubender Eleganz und angenehmer Behaglichkeit. Hotelier André Balazs (u. a. auch Besitzer des Chateau Marmont in L.A.) und der französische Designer Christian Liaigre haben mit ihrem wohltuend modernistischen Interieur die perfekte Kulisse für ihre schillernde Klientel geschaffen. Die Lobby ist einer der angesagtesten Treffpunkte der Stadt – ein öffentliches Wohnzimmer, in dem man in Ruhe einen Kaffee trinken, aber auch bis zwei Uhr morgens mit Freunden feiern kann. Das aufmerksame Personal lässt keine Wünsche offen: Man packt Ihnen sogar die Koffer, wenn die Rückkehr in den schnöden Alltag ansteht.

Le Mercer pourrait bien être le petit hôtel new-yorkais idéal. L'élégant bâtiment en brique à la façade ornée fut construit en 1890 par William Schickel, l'architecte de plusieurs édifices religieux à Manhattan. Il avait été conçu pour abriter les bureaux de l'une des plus grandes familles de New York, les Astor. Bien placé à un croisement au cœur de SoHo, il réussit le tour de force d'être ultra-chic tout en étant douillet et accueillant. L'hôtelier André Balazs (qui possède aussi, entre autres, le Château Marmont à Los Angeles) et le décorateur français Christian Liaigre ont créé un décor moderniste et apaisant, parfaite toile de fond pour une clientèle haute en couleur. Le lobby est l'un des lieux les plus courus de New York : un salon où l'on peut se lover dans un coin devant un café ou faire la fête avec des amis jusqu'à deux heures du matin. Le personnel attentif peut tout faire, même préparer vos valises quand viendra le moment de retourner à la dure réalité.

Preiskategorie: $$$$.
Zimmer: 75 Luxuszimmer, davon 4 Suiten und 2 Lofts.
Restaurants: The Mercer Kitchen: moderne Küche von Jean-Georges Vongerichten, Frühstück, Lunch, Dinner. **The Lobby:** 24 Stunden geöffnet. **subMercer:** Bar im Keller, Mi–Sa (23–4 Uhr) geöffnet.
Geschichte: Das sechsgeschossige neoromanische Gebäude aus dem Jahr 1890 wurde 1998 zum Hotel umgebaut und eröffnet.
X-Faktor: Die superluxuriösen Bäder sind 30 m² groß – und damit größer als die meisten New Yorker Hotelzimmer. Die riesigen Marmorwannen bieten zwei (oder mehr) Personen Platz.

Catégorie de prix : $$$$.
Chambres : 75 chambres luxueuses dont 4 suites et 2 lofts.
Restauration : The Mercer Kitchen, cuisine contemporaine du chef Jean-Georges Vongerichten ; petit-déjeuner, déjeuner, dîner. **The Lobby,** ouvert 24h/24. **subMercer,** bar en sous-sol ; ouvert Mer–Sam (23h–4h).
Histoire : Le bâtiment néo-roman de six étages fut construit en 1890 et converti en hôtel en 1998.
Le « petit plus » : Les salles de bain super luxe font 30 mètres carrés. Leurs baignoires peuvent accueillirent deux personnes, voire plus.

SIXTY SoHo

60 Thompson Street, New York, NY 10012
☎ +1 877 431 0400 ☐ +1 212 431 0200
info@sixtyhotels.com
www.sixtyhotels.com/soho

Subway: Spring Street (C,E), Canal Street (A, C, E,1),
Prince Street (R, W)

This discreet SoHo hideaway is the flagship of young-turk hotelier Jason Pomeranc's. Opened in 2001, SIXTY SoHo, formerly 60 Thompson belongs to the first wave of boutique hotels in this area, and it's settled in to become a well-known neighborhood landmark. Thompson Street is a quiet SoHo side-street lined with shops and some great restaurants – Japanese gem Omen Azen is across the street. 60 Thompson's fun rooftop bar, A60, is only open to members and guests, and it attracts a typical downtown clientele, chic and connected. After drinks, drift down to the hotel's restaurant, Kittichai, which earns critical raves even from picky New York food critics for its delicious contemporary Thai cuisine. When you finally call it a night and retreat into your room (designed by Thomas O'Brien, the guru of "warm modernism") with its marble-tiled baths, wood floors, brown leather headboards and 400-thread-count SFERRA sheets, you'll rest comfortably knowing you've really experienced the best of SoHo.

Price category: $$$$.
Rooms: 97 rooms, 10 balcony suites including a two-bedroom, duplex SIXTY loft.
Restaurants: Kittichai, contemporary Thai cuisine, breakfast, lunch, dinner. **Thom Bar,** cocktails and bar menu, 5pm–2am. **A60,** rooftop lounge, cocktails, 6pm–12:30am (closed during winter).
History: Opened 2001, renovated 2005.
X-Factor: The rooms have pantries stocked with goodies from nearby gourmet shop Dean & Deluca.

Dieses diskrete Refugium in SoHo ist das Flaggschiff der Thompson-Gruppe des jungen aufstrebenden Hoteliers Jason Pomeranc (Hollywood Roosevelt Hotel, Thompson Beverly Hills). Das 2001 als eines der ersten Boutiquehotels in diesem Teil der Stadt unter dem Namen 60 Thompson eröffnete heutige SIXTY SoHo, zählt inzwischen zu den bekannten Wahrzeichen des Viertels. Die Thompson Street ist eine ruhige, von kleinen Geschäften und erstklassigen Restaurants gesäumte Seitenstraße – schräg gegenüber liegt das japanische Kleinod Omen Azen. Die Dachbar A60 ist Mitgliedern und Hotelgästen vorbehalten und lockt die schicke Downtown-Klientel an. Nach ein paar Cocktails geht es hinunter zum Hotelrestaurant Kittichai, das sogar die verwöhnten New Yorker Kritiker mit exzellenter Thai-Küche begeistert. Und nach einer langen Nacht zieht man sich in die von Thomas O'Brien (dem Guru des „warmen Modernismus") gestalteten Zimmer mit Marmorbädern und Holzböden zurück und ruht in Betten mit braunen, lederbespannten Kopfteilen, die mit feinsten SFERRA-Bezügen zum Träumen einladen – wahrlich das Beste von SoHo.

Ce discret refuge dans une rue tranquille de SoHo bordée de boutiques et de bonnes tables (le japonais Omen Azen se trouve en face) est le fleuron du jeune-turc de l'hôtellerie, Jason Pomeranc. Inauguré en 2001, SIXYT SoHo, anciennement 60 Thompson, appartient à la première vague des hôtels boutiques du quartier dont il est devenu l'un des hauts lieux. Le A60, son bar sur le toit réservé aux clients et aux membres, attire une clientèle chic et branchée très « Downtown ». Après un cocktail, descendez au restaurant Kittichai, dont la cuisine thaïlandaise contemporaine ravit les critiques gastronomiques les plus exigeants de New York. Une fois repu, vous pourrez vous retirer dans votre chambre décorée par le gourou du « modernisme chaleureux », Thomas O'Brien, avec sa salle de bain en marbre, son parquet, sa tête de lit en cuir et ses draps de chez SFERRA. Vous dormirez tranquille en sachant que vous avez vécu ce qu'il y a de mieux à SoHo.

Preiskategorie: $$$$.
Zimmer: 97 Gästezimmer, 10 Balkonsuiten, davon ein Duplex-SIXTY-Loft mit zwei Schlafzimmern.
Restaurants: Kittichai: moderne Thai-Küche, Frühstück, Lunch, Dinner. Thom Bar: Cocktails und Bar-Menu, geöffnet 17–2 Uhr. A60: Dach-Lounge, Cocktails, geöffnet 18–0.30 Uhr (im Winter geschlossen).
Geschichte: 2001 eröffnet, 2014 renoviert.
X-Faktor: Die Pantry-Küchen der Zimmer sind mit Köstlichkeiten des nahen Delikatessengeschäfts Dean & Deluca bestückt.

Catégorie de prix : $$$$.
Chambres : 97 chambres, 10 suites avec balcon dont un loft en duplex avec deux chambres.
Restauration : Kittichai, cuisine thaïlandaise contemporaine ; petit-déjeuner, déjeuner et dîner. Thom Bar, cocktails et en-cas ; 17h–2h. A60, bar en terrasse, cocktails ; 18h–0h30 (fermé en hiver).
Histoire : Inauguré en 2001, rénové en 2014.
Le « petit plus » : Les chambres sont équipées de garde-manger remplis de délices provenant de chez Dean & Deluca, la boutique gastronomique voisine.

The SoHo Grand Hotel

310 West Broadway, New York, NY 10013
☎ +1 212 965 3000   ☐ +1 212 965 3244
reservations@sohogrand.com
www.sohogrand.com
Subway: Canal Street (A, C, E, 1)

Back in the 1800s, this was a neighborhood of solid and regal factory buildings with intricately ornamented cast iron facades. Blighted and neglected for decades, these buildings got colonized by New York painters, sculptors, and performing artists in the 1970s. The gallery scene has mostly moved on, eateries and boutiques have moved in, but SoHo's arty history and urban industrial chic still draw visitors to its narrow, cobblestoned streets. The SoHo Grand Hotel, opened in 1996, was the neighborhood's first hotel, and it's mellowed into a downtown classic. Interior designer William Sofield uses a simple palette of neutral beiges and grays, with quirky accents like a staircase made with glass bottle insets. His quiet design's a perfect backdrop for the colorful parade of locals and international travelers who come to stay (or just sip a Martini) in "SoHo's Living Room".

Price category: $$.
Rooms: 353 doubles, 10 suites and 2 penthouse loft suites.
Restaurants: All contemporary American food: **The Club Room,** breakfast, lunch, dinner, brunch. **Grand Bar & Lounge** ("SoHo's Living Room"), appetizers, drinks from midday. **The Yard,** dinner, drinks, open May-September.
History: Opened in 1996, the building was designed and constructed by architect David Helpern.
X-Factor: One of the few pet-friendly hotels in New York City. If you don't bring your pet, the hotel can provide an in-room goldfish.

Im 19. Jahrhundert bestand SoHo vorrangig aus massiven, stattlichen Fabrikbauten mit kunstvoll verzierten Gusseisenfassaden. Nach jahrzehntelanger Verwahrlosung wurden die Gebäude in den 1970er Jahren von New Yorker Malern, Bildhauern und Künstlern wiederentdeckt. Obwohl die Kunstszene inzwischen Restaurants und Boutiquen Platz gemacht hat, zieht SoHos unkonventionelles, historisch-urbanes Industrieflair weiterhin zahlreiche Besucher in die schmalen Pflasterstraßen. Das 1996 eröffnete SoHo Grand Hotel (der erste Hotelneubau im Viertel seit über 100 Jahren) hat sich zu einem Downtown-Klassiker entwickelt. Innenarchitekt William Sofield verwendete neutrale Beige- und Grautöne und setzte mit ungewöhnlichen Bauelementen – z. B. einer Lochgittertreppe mit eingelassenen Flaschenböden – eigenwillige Akzente. Sein ruhiges Design bildet den perfekten Hintergrund für die bunte Szene lokaler und internationaler Gäste, die sich in „SoHos Wohnzimmer" niederlassen – auch um nur einen Martini zu trinken.

Au 19ᵉ siècle, ce quartier abritait des usines rutilantes aux façades en fonte ouvragées. Négligées durant des décennies, envahies par la rouille, elles furent colonisées dans les années 1970 par des peintres, des artistes et des sculpteurs. Puis vinrent les galeries qui cédèrent ensuite le pas aux restaurants et aux boutiques, mais le côté bohème de SoHo et son chic industriel urbain continuent d'attirer les visiteurs dans ses rues étroites et pavées. Inauguré en 1996, le SoHo Grand Hotel fut le premier hôtel du quartier et est désormais devenu un classique. Le décorateur William Sofield a utilisé une palette simple de tons neutres beige et gris avec quelques touches excentriques telles que l'escalier en bouteilles de verre. Son décor discret convient parfaitement au défilé coloré des voyageurs internationaux et des habitants du quartier, venus prendre une chambre ou un martini dans « le salon de SoHo ».

Preiskategorie: $$.
Zimmer: 353 Doppelzimmer, 10 Suiten und 2 Penthouse-Loft-Suiten.
Restaurants: Moderne amerikanische Küche. **The Club Room:** Frühstück, Lunch, Dinner, Brunch. **Grand Bar & Lounge** („SoHos Wohnzimmer"): Snacks, Drinks ab 12 Uhr. **The Yard:** Dinner, Drinks, Mai–September geöffnet.
Geschichte: Das Gebäude wurde 1996 vom Architekten David Helpern entworfen und als erstes Boutiquehotel in SoHo errichtet.
X-Faktor: Eines der wenigen tierfreundlichen Hotels in New York City.

Catégorie de prix : $$.
Chambres : 353 chambres doubles, 10 suites et 2 suites en loft-penthouse.
Restauration : Cuisine américaine contemporaire : **The Club Room,** petit-déjeuner, déjeuner et dîner, brunch. **Grand Bar & Lounge** (« le salon de SoHo »), mises en bouche et drinks à partir de midi. **The Yard,** dîner, drinks ; ouvert de mai à septembre.
Histoire : Ouvert en 1996, le bâtiment a été conçu par l'architecte David Helpern. Ce fut le premier hôtel boutique à ouvrir à SoHo.
Le « petit plus » : Un des rares hôtels de New York qui accepte les animaux.

The Maritime Hotel

363 West 16th Street, New York, NY 10011
☎ +1 212 242 4300   📄 +1 212 242 1188
www.themaritimehotel.com
Subway: 8th Avenue (L), 14th Street (A, C, E)

Famed New Orleans architect Albert Ledner designed this soaring tower of white ceramic tile and porthole windows for the National Maritime Union in 1964. Not all New Yorkers were happy with Ledner's "eccentric Modernist" creation – with its wall of signature round porthole windows, the building was compared to a beached ocean liner that washed up on a Manhattan street. But over the years, people grew fond of the big ship, and in 2003, The Maritime Hotel was beautifully transformed by hotelier-designers Sean MacPherson, Eric Goode, Richard Born and Ira Drukier. Today it's a landmark and a center of activity for the style-setters and arty types who congregate in New York's Chelsea and Meatpacking districts. It's more like an island oasis than a hotel: inside, there's a 10,000-square-foot open garden, inspired by Brazilian landscape architect Roberto Burle Marx, and a half dozen leafy magnolia trees. Unpretentious, consistent and fun, with fantastic restaurants and a marvelous, attentive staff, The Maritime Hotel is fast becoming a New York must.

Price category: $$$.
Rooms: 121 rooms and 5 penthouse suites
Restaurants: La Bottega, breakfast, lunch, dinner, 24 hour room service, rustic Italian. **Tao Downtown**, Asian cuisine, dinner.
Cabanas, bar on the roof
History: Building completed in 1964, renovated in 2003. Before it became the Maritime, the building was a dormitory for sailors.
X-Factor: You can rent a bike from the hotel desk to explore Chelsea, the Meatpacking District and Manhattan like a local.

Das skurrile weiße Gebäude mit Keramikfassade und Bullaugenfenstern wurde 1964 vom Architekten Albert Ledner aus New Orleans für die National Maritime Union entworfen. Ledners „exzentrisch modernistischer" Bau mit seinen charakteristischen Bullaugen gefiel damals nicht allen New Yorkern, die ihn gern mit einem mitten in Manhattan gestrandeten Ozeandampfer verglichen. Aber mit den Jahren schloss die Stadt das große Schiff ins Herz. 2003 wurde das Hotel von Sean MacPherson, Eric Goode, Richard Born and Ira Drukier einem Team aus Hoteliers und Designern wunderschön umgestaltet. Heute ist es Wahrzeichen und Treffpunkt für alle Trendsetter und Kulturschaffenden im Stadtteil Chelsea und dem sogenannten "Meatpacking District". Das Maritime ist eher Inseloase als Hotel – im Innenhof stößt man auf einen vom brasilianischen Landschaftsarchitekten Roberto Burle Marx inspirierten Garten samt Magnolienbäumen. Unprätentiös, stimmig und verspielt, mit fantastischen Restaurants und vorbildlichem Personal entwickelt sich das Maritime zu einem New Yorker Muss.

Le célèbre architecte néo-orléanais Albert Ledner a conçu cette haute tour en plaques de céramique blanche aux fenêtres en forme de hublots pour la National Maritime Union en 1964. À l'époque, ce bâtiment « moderniste excentrique » aux fenêtres en hublot fut sévèrement critiqué et comparé à un paquebot échoué dans une rue de Manhattan. Au fil des ans, les New-Yorkais s'y sont attachés et, en 2003, il fut magnifiquement reconverti par les hôteliers Sean MacPherson, Eric Goode, Richard Born and Ira Drukier. Sans prétention et amusant, c'est aujourd'hui le lieu de rendez-vous des branchés et des bobos à Chelsea et Meatpacking District. Ses 930 mètres carrés de jardin inspiré du paysagiste brésilien Roberto Burle Max et ses six magnolias touffus en font une oasis au cœur de la ville. Avec ses excellents restaurants et son personnel chaleureux et attentif, le Maritime est en passe de devenir un must à New York.

Preiskategorie: $$$.
Zimmer: 121 Zimmer und 5 Penthouse-Suiten.
Restaurants: La Bottega: rustikale italienische Küche, Frühstück, Mittag- und Abendessen, 24 Stunden Zimmerservice. **Tao Downtown:** asiatische Küche, Abendessen. **Cabanas:** Bar auf dem Dach.
Geschichte: Das Gebäude wurde 1964 fertiggestellt und 2003 umfassend renoviert und als Hotel eröffnet. Vor seiner Umwandlung war das Maritime ein Seemannsheim.
X-Faktor: Man kann an der Rezeption ein Fahrrad leihen, um Chelsea und Manhattan wie die Einheimischen zu erkunden.

Catégorie de prix : $$$.
Chambres : 121 chambres et 5 suites en penthouse.
Restauration : La Bottega, petit-déjeuner, déjeuner et dîner, service 24h/24, cuisine rustique italienne. **Tao Downtown,** cuisine asiatique, dîner. **Cabanas,** bar sur le toit.
Histoire : Le bâtiment a été achevé en 1964 et restauré en 2003. Avant de devenir le Maritime, il a accueilli des dortoirs pour marins.
Le « petit plus » : On peut louer des bicyclettes à la réception pour explorer Chelsea le Meatpacking District et Manhattan comme un vrai New-Yorkais.

LOTTO

CIGARETTES

MINTS

ASPIRIN

NEWSPAPERS

TOOTHPASTE

CANDY

BAND AIDS

MAGAZINES

RAZORS

SHAVE CREAM

terax SHAMP Latte

terax SHAMP Latte

ORIGINAL

MASON PEARSON
London. England.
HAIR BRUSH

MASON PEARSON
London. England.
HAIR BRUSH

TRIM

The Greenwich Hotel

377 Greenwich Street, New York, NY 10013
☎ +1 212 941 8900   📠 +1 212 941 8600
reservations@thegreenwichhotel.com
www.thegreenwichhotel.com
Subway: Franklin (1), Chambers Street (1, 2, 3)

Actor Robert De Niro is the Godfather behind the renaissance of New York's Tribeca (Triangle Below Canal Street), the waterfront loft area tucked between SoHo and the Financial District. He moved his offices to this old warehouse neighborhood in the 1980s, opened the Tribeca Grill restaurant, founded the Tribeca film festival, and in 2008 he launched The Greenwich Hotel, a small, private hotel next door to the restaurant. The eight-story modern building is all new, and Grayling Design's interiors are super-cozy, with natural wood floors, and warm artisan touches like bathrooms decorated with handmade Moroccan tiles. You can really feel the De Niro signature everywhere in the masculine, Italian atmosphere, lightened throughout by beautiful flower arrangements. The suites are designed to resemble artist's ateliers, two of them with 30-foot skylights, chef's kitchens, and stone fireplaces. All in all, this makes an exceptional hideaway in one of New York's most interesting neighborhoods; you'll feel as if you've stepped into a scene from "The Godfather II".

Price category: $$$$.
Rooms: 88 rooms including 12 suites and a penthouse, no two rooms alike.
Restaurants: Locanda Verde, casual Italian tavern, breakfast, lunch, dinner.
History: Newly built and opened in 2008.
X-Factor: Guests have exclusive access to the hotel's spectacular Shibui Spa, designed by Mikio Shinagawa, which incorporates an original 250-year-old Japanese wood-and-bamboo farmhouse.

Robert De Niro stand Pate für die Renaissance von Tribeca (Triangle Below Canal Street), dem am Hudson zwischen SoHo und dem Financial District gelegenen Viertel. In den 1980ern verlegte er sein Büro in die damalige Lagerhallen-Gegend, eröffnete das Restaurant Tribeca Grill, gründete das Tribeca Film Festival und baute 2008 direkt neben dem Restaurant das kleine, intime Greenwich Hotel. Das achtgeschossige moderne Gebäude wurde von Grayling Design supergemütlich ausgestattet: Holzböden und viel Kunsthandwerk – z. B. handgemachte marokkanische Fliesen in den Bädern – sorgen für eine warme Atmosphäre. Jedes Detail des Hotels mit seinem maskulin-italienischen Charme, aufgehellt durch viele Blumenarrangements, trägt De Niros Handschrift. Die Suiten erinnern an Künstlerateliers, zwei davon haben neun Meter hohe Dachfenster und bieten voll ausgestattete Küchen und offene Kamine. Das Greenwich ist ein außergewöhnliches Hotel in einem der interessantesten Viertel New Yorks – und man kommt sich vor wie in einer Szene von „Der Pate II".

Robert De Niro est le parrain de la résurrection de Tribeca, ce quartier d'entrepôts au bord du fleuve, coincé entre SoHo et le Financial District. Il y a installé ses bureaux dans les années 1980, a ouvert le restaurant Tribeca Grill, fondé le festival de cinéma de Tribeca et, en 2008, a inauguré le Greenwich, un petit hôtel intime attenant au restaurant. Le bâtiment de huit étages flambant neuf et décoré par Grayling Design est un vrai nid douillet, avec des parquets en bois naturel et de belles touches artisanales telles que les carreaux marocains faits à la main dans les salles de bain. On sent la patte de De Niro dans l'atmosphère masculine et italienne, agrémentée de superbes bouquets partout. Les suites sont conçues comme des ateliers d'artiste, deux ont des verrières de neuf mètres de haut, des cuisines pour cordon bleu et des cheminées en pierre. C'est un havre exceptionnel dans un des quartiers les plus interéssants de Manhattan. On se croirait dans une scène du « Parrain II ».

Preiskategorie: $$$$.
Zimmer: 88 Zimmer, davon 12 Suiten und ein Penthouse. Alle Zimmer sind individuell gestaltet.
Restaurants: Locanda Verde: gemütliche italienische Trattoria um die Ecke, Frühstück, Lunch und Dinner.
Geschichte: 2008 neu erbaut und eröffnet.
X-Faktor: Das Shibui Spa, der einzigartige, von Mikio Shinagawa entworfene Wellnessbereich, ist den Hotelgästen vorbehalten. In das Spa wurde ein echtes, 250 Jahre altes japanisches Bauernhaus wieder aufgebaut.

Catégorie de prix : $$$$.
Chambres : 88 chambres dont 12 suites et un penthouse. Toutes les chambres sont différentes.
Restauration : Locanda Verde, taverne italienne de quartier sans prétentions, petit-déjeuner, déjeuner et dîner.
Histoire : Immeuble récent inauguré en 2008.
Le « petit plus » : Le spectaculaire spa Shibui, réservé aux clients de l'hôtel, conçu par Mikio Shinagawa et dans lequel une ferme japonaise vieille de 250 ans en bois et bambou a été reconstruite.

The Bowery Hotel

335 Bowery, New York, NY 10003
☎ +1 212 505 9100   📠 +1 212 505 9700
info@bohonyc.com
www.theboweryhotel.com

Subway: Bleecker Street (6), Broadway-Lafayette Street (B, D, F, V)

The Bowery is a name that, for a native New Yorker of a certain age, conjures up images of seedy flophouses and Salvation Army missions. More recently, in the 1970s and 1980s, the Bowery was the white-hot center of downtown hip, with New Wave and Punk bands like the Ramones and Talking Heads, and artists like Jean-Michel Basquiat lurking in this street's dark, gritty, but artistically fascinating shadows. The Bowery Hotel, opened in 2007, is a first-rate luxury hotel that nevertheless manages to feel connected in both design and spirit with the neighborhood's Bohemian past. Designers and owners Eric Goode and Sean MacPherson have created a warm, funky boho loft-away-from-home look, a mix of urban architectural salvage and relaxed, thrift shop finds. The rooms have iron industrial-style windows and faded Oriental rugs. When you enter the lobby, overstuffed velvet chairs and a roaring fire await. Bohemia never felt so cozy.

Price category: $$$.
Rooms: 135 rooms including 25 suites.
Restaurants: Gemma, rustic Italian cuisine, breakfast, lunch, dinner.
Bowery Lobby Bar, open 5pm–2am.
History: Opened 2007, building constructed 2004. This architecturally nondescript 16-story tower was built on the site of a former parking garage in this once-edgy neighborhood of rock bars and flophouses. The new owners renovated it completely, inside and out.
X-Factor: Each room has an authentic Turkish Oushak rug, and endless views of lower Manhattan.

The Bowery ist ein Begriff, der bei vielen New Yorkern Bilder von schäbigen Absteigen und Heilsarmee-Missionen hervorruft. In den 1970ern und 1980ern bildete diese Gegend das Zentrum der Downtown-Szene, mit New Wave und Punk Bands wie den Ramones und den Talking Heads und Künstlern wie Jean-Michel Basquiat, die in den dunklen, harten, aber künstlerisch faszinierenden Schatten der Bowery herumlungerten. Das 2007 eröffnete Bowery Hotel ist ein echtes Luxushotel, dem es jedoch gelingt, Reminiszenzen an das Design und die unkonventionelle, aufregende Vergangenheit des Viertels zu erzeugen. Die Designer und Eigentümer Eric Goode und Sean MacPherson haben einen einladenden, lässigen Loft-Look entwickelt, eine Mischung aus urbanen, historischen Baustoffen und entspanntem Secondhand-Schick. Die Zimmer haben eiserne Sprossenfenster und verblasste, antike Orientteppiche, und in der Lobby erwarten den Gast üppig gepolsterte Samtsessel und ein knisterndes Kaminfeuer. Nie zuvor war das Bohemeleben so warm und behaglich.

Pour les New-Yorkais d'un certain âge, le « Bowery » évoque des images de SDF et de foyers de l'Armée du salut. Dans les années 1970 et 80, des groupes punk et new age comme les Ramones ou les Talking Heads ainsi que des artistes tels que Jean-Michel Basquiat redonnèrent à ses rues sombres mais artistiquement chargées leurs lettres de noblesse. Inauguré en 2007, le Bowery Hotel est un hôtel de luxe de premier ordre qui respecte, par son esprit et son esthétique, le passé bohème du quartier. Les propriétaires et designers Eric Goode et Sean MacPherson ont créé un lieu chaleureux, décontracté et dans le vent, mélange de récupération d'architecture urbaine et de trouvailles de brocantes. Les chambres ont des fenêtres à croisillons en fer et de vieux tapis d'Orient. Dans le hall, de confortables fauteuils en velours vous attendent devant un grand feu de cheminée. La vie de bohème n'a jamais été aussi douillette.

Preiskategorie: $$$.
Zimmer: 135 Zimmer, davon 25 Suiten.
Restaurants: Gemma: rustikale italienische Küche, Frühstück, Lunch, Dinner. **Bowery Lobby Bar:** 17–2 Uhr geöffnet.
Geschichte: Das architektonisch unauffällige 16-geschossige Gebäude wurde 2004 auf dem Gelände eines Parkhauses erbaut. 2007 haben die neuen Eigentümer den Bau vollständig umbauen lassen.
X-Faktor: Jedes Zimmer bietet einen original türkischen Uschak-Teppich sowie deckenhohe Industriefenster mit wunderbarem Blick auf Lower Manhattan.

Catégorie de prix : $$$.
Chambres : 135 chambres dont 25 suites.
Restauration : Gemma, cuisine italienne rustique ; petit-déjeuner, déjeuner et dîner. **Bowery Lobby Bar,** ouvert 17h–2h.
Histoire : La tour, architecturalement quelconque, a été construite en 2004 sur le site d'un ancien parking dans ce quartier autrefois malfamé qui accueillaient des boîtes de rock et des asiles de nuit. Les nouveaux propriétaires l'ont intégralement réaménagée.
Le « petit plus » : Les chambres sont équipées d'un authentique tapis turc Oushak et offrent des vues imprenables sur le sud de Manhattan.

GEMMA

Cum Grano Salis

FRUTTI DI MARE

TRATTORIA

SPIRITI

PANE E VINO

GELATI

Lafayette House

38 East 4th Street, New York, NY 10003
☎ +1 212 505 8100   ⬛ +1 212 505 2700
info@lafayettenyc.com
www.lafayettenyc.com

Subway: Bleecker Street (6), Broadway-Lafayette Street (B, D, F, V)

The Lafayette House is the sort of low-key, nicely appointed small hotel that's a commonplace in Paris or London, but a rarity in New York. There's no lobby or reception, when you check in, you buzz the door and an employee appears with your key. (Warning: there's no elevator or porter, either.) Hoteliers Eric Goode and Sean MacPherson renovated and decorated this 19th century five-story rowhouse; it is a quieter, more apartment-like alternative to their nearby Bowery Hotel. The shabby-chic rooms, some with kitchenettes and terraces, drip with carefully-assembled Victoriana: brocaded fabrics, striped wallpaper, crystal chandeliers, and velvet curtains. (Rooms no. 5 and 6 also have 14 foot ceilings.) The Lafayette House enjoys one of the best downtown locations for shopping, nightlife, and dining — it straddles the border of Greenwich Village and SoHo, and it's only a five minute skip to Nolita, the very cool enclave of boutiques, shoe shops (Sigerson Morrison, Otto Tootsi Plohound) and bars just south of East Houston Street.

Price category: $$$.
Rooms: 15 rooms including 8 suites.
Restaurants: None but room service can be ordered from the nearby B Bar and Grill. Tea and coffee can be made in the rooms.
History: 1848 rowhouse renovated in 2007 by hoteliers Eric Goode and Sean MacPherson.
X-Factor: You feel like you're staying in your own apartment, not a hotel, and every room has a working gas fireplace.

Lafayette House ist eines dieser kleinen Hotels, die man in Paris oder London häufig findet, in New York aber nur selten. Es gibt keine Lobby oder Rezeption – stattdessen klingelt man an der Tür, und schon erscheint ein Angestellter mit dem Zimmerschlüssel. (Achtung: Es gibt weder Aufzug noch Gepäckträger.) Das fünfgeschossige Haus aus dem 19. Jahrhundert wurde von Eric Goode und Sean MacPherson renoviert und ist eine ruhigere Alternative zu ihrem nahen Bowery Hotel. Die eleganten Zimmer, einige mit Kitchenette und Terrasse, wurden mit Brokatstoffen, gestreiften Tapeten, Kristalllüstern und Samtvorhängen bewusst auf leicht angegilbten Viktorianismus getrimmt. Mit seiner Lage direkt an der Grenze zwischen Greenwich Village und SoHo ist das Lafayette House der ideale Ausgangspunkt für Shopping, Nachtleben und die Restaurants von Downtown. Auch die coolen Boutiquen, Schuhgeschäfte (Sigerson Morrison, Otto Tootsi Plohound) und Bars von Nolita direkt südlich der East Houston Street sind nur fünf Minuten entfernt.

Le Lafayette House est un petit hôtel de charme comme on en trouve à Londres et à Paris mais rarement à New York. Il n'y a ni hall ni réception ; à votre arrivée, vous sonnez à la porte et un employé apparaît avec votre clef. (Attention, pas d'ascenseur ni de porteur non plus.) Eric Goode et Sean MacPherson ont rénové cette maison particulière du 19e siècle de cinq étages comme une alternative plus intime au Bowery voisin. Les chambres shabby chic, certaines équipées d'une kitchenette et d'une terrasse, regorgent d'antiquités victoriennes soigneusement choisies : brocards, papier peint à rayures, lustres en cristal, rideaux en velours. (Les n° 5 et 6 ont une hauteur de plafond de 4,30 mètres). Le Lafayette est idéalement situé pour le shopping, la vie nocturne et les restaurants ; à cheval entre Greenwich Village et SoHo, il n'est qu'à deux pas de Nolita, au sud d'East Houston Street, avec ses boutiques branchées, ses magasins de chaussures (Sigerson Morrison, Otto Tootsi Plohound) et ses bars.

Preiskategorie: $$$.
Zimmer: 15 Zimmer, davon 8 Suiten.
Restaurant: Keines – aber per Zimmerservice kann im nahe gelegenen B Bar and Grill bestellt werden. Tee und Kaffee lassen sich auf dem Zimmer zubereiten.
Geschichte: Das ehemalige Reihenhaus aus dem Jahre 1848 wurde 2007 von den Hoteliers Eric Goode und Sean MacPherson renoviert.
X-Faktor: Man fühlt sich nicht wie im Hotel, sondern wie in einer Wohnung, und jedes Zimmer verfügt über einen funktionstüchtigen Gaskamin.

Catégorie de prix : $$$.
Chambres : 15 chambres dont 8 suites.
Restauration : Pas de cuisine mais on peut se faire livrer des plats depuis le B Bar and Grill voisin. On peut préparer son café et son thé dans les chambres.
Histoire : Maison particulière datant de 1848 et restaurée en 2007 par les hôteliers Eric Goode et Sean MacPherson.
Le « petit plus » : Vous n'avez pas l'impression d'être à l'hôtel mais chez vous. Chaque chambre possède une cheminée fonctionnant au gaz.

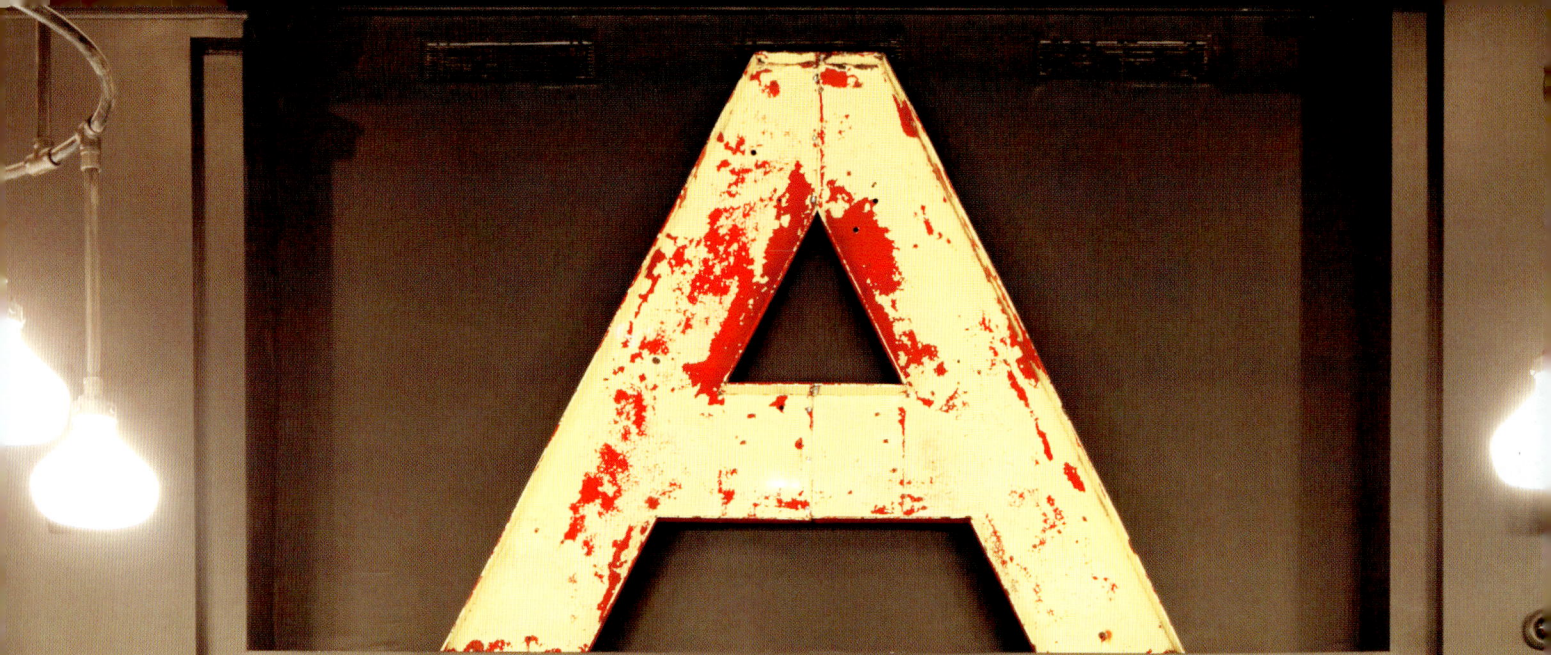

Ace Hotel

20 W 29th Street, New York City, NY 10001
☎ +1 212 679 2222　☐ +1 212 679 1947
enquire.nyc@acehotel.com
www.acehotel.com/newyork

Subway: 28th Street (N, R)

Alex Calderwood, the now deceased co-founder of the
Ace hotel chain, accompanied rock bands on tour for many
years. His concept for the perfect hotel is rooted in this
period, and was further refined over the years. In an Ace
hotel, you mustn't expect luxury in the traditional sense –
instead you get bags of originality. No two rooms are the
same, and those in the upper price bracket boast acoustic
guitars, Smeg refrigerators, and turntables. Guests with lots
of potential but a meagre budget are also welcome, as there
are a few rooms with bunk beds as well. The Ace Hotel is
located in Midtown on Broadway, from where you can see
the Empire State Building. However the bustling life of
central Manhattan disappears as soon as you enter the lobby
of the Ace Hotel, because guests are intent on communing
with their laptops. The cafeteria is first rate, as are the bar
and restaurant – try the burger made with minced lamb.

Price category: $$$.
Rooms: 280, eight of which are Loft Suites.
Restaurants: The Breslin Bar & Dining Room, John Dory Oyster Bar,
Bar: Lobby Bar till 2 am, Breslin Bar till 4 am.
History: The 11-storey hotel was built in 1904. Until 2008 it was
the Breslin Hotel, latterly a hostel for long-term guests. This is an Ace
family tradition: the first hotel in the chain, which opened in Seattle in
1999, was a converted night-time shelter.
X-Factor: There is a branch of Stumptown Coffee Roasters from
Portland in the lobby, selling what is regarded as the best (and
strongest!) coffee in New York.

Alex Calderwood, ein inzwischen verstorbener Gründer der Ace-Gruppe, hat jahrelang Rockbands auf Tourneen begleitet. Sein Konzept für ein ideales Hotel stammt aus dieser Zeit und wurde über die Jahre noch weiter verfeinert. Im Ace Hotel darf man keinen klassischen Luxus erwarten, dafür reichlich Originalität. Kein Zimmer gleicht dem anderen, in solchen der oberen Kategorie stehen Akustikgitarren, Smeg-Kühlschränke und Schallplattenspieler bereit, und selbst Gäste mit viel Potenzial, aber wenig Budget sind willkommen, denn es gibt auch ein paar Zimmer mit Doppelstockbett. Das Ace Hotel steht in Midtown am Broadway. Das Empire State Building steht in Sichtweite. Vom umtriebigen Leben in der Mitte Manhattans ist aber bereits in der Lobby des Ace Hotel nichts mehr zu spüren, weil die Gäste die innere Einkehr vor ihren Laptops praktizieren. Die Cafeteria ist erstklassig, die Bar und das Restaurant auch – probieren Sie den Burger mit gehacktem Lammfleisch!

Alex Calderwood, l'un des fondateurs aujourd'hui décédé du groupe Ace, a accompagné pendant des années des groupes de rock en tournée. Sa conception de l'hôtel idéal date de cette époque et a été affinée au fil des ans. À l'hôtel Ace, mieux vaut ne pas attendre de luxe classique, mais bien plus de l'originalité en abondance. Toutes les chambres sont différentes, dans celles de la catégorie supérieure on trouve des guitares acoustiques, des réfrigérateurs Smeg et des tourne-disques et même les clients au fort potentiel mais au petit budget sont les bienvenus car quelques chambres ont des lits superposés. L'hôtel Ace est situé au cœur de Broadway, l'Empire State Building à portée de vue. Dès le hall de l'hôtel, on ne ressent cependant plus rien de l'activité trépidante du centre de Manhattan car les clients pratiquent la méditation face à leurs ordinateurs portables. La cafétéria est de toute première classe, le bar et le restaurant aussi – essayez le burger à la viande d'agneau hachée !

Preiskategorie: $$$.
Zimmer: 280, davon acht Loft Suiten.
Restaurants: The Breslin Bar & Dining Room, John Dory Oyster Bar
Bar: Lobby Bar bis 2 Uhr, The Breslin Bar bis 4 Uhr
Geschichte: Das elfstöckige Gebäude wurde im Jahr 1904 erbaut. Bis 2008 befand sich darin das Breslin Hotel, zuletzt eine Herberge mit Langzeitgästen. In der Ace-Familie hat das Tradition: Das erste Haus, in Seattle, entstand dort 1999 aus einem Nachtasyl.
X-Faktor: In der Lobby befindet sich eine Filiale von Stumptown Coffee Roasters aus Portland, deren Kaffee als der beste (und kräftigste!) in New York gilt.

Catégorie de prix : $$$.
Chambres : 280, dont 8 suites loft.
Restauration : The Breslin Bar & Dining Room, John Dory Oyster Bar,
Bar : Dans le foyer jusqu'à 2 h, The Breslin Bar jusqu'à 4 h.
Histoire : L'immeuble de onze étages a été construit en 1904. Il a abrité le Breslin Hotel jusqu'en 2008, puis un gîte pour séjours de longue durée. C'est une tradition dans la famille Ace : la première maison, à Seattle, ouverte en 1999 faisait suite à un asile de nuit.
Le « petit plus » : Dans le hall se trouve une filiale de Stumptown Coffee Roasters de Portland, dont le café est considéré comme le meilleur (et le plus fort !) de New York.

SOMEONE
WHO HAS
READ MON
TAIGNE
MARVELS
AT NOTHING
M LIFSHITZ

everything is going to be alright

Gramercy Park Hotel

2 Lexington Avenue, New York, NY 10010
☎ +1 212 920 3300   📇 +1 212 673 5890
reservations@gramercyparkhotel.com
www.gramercyparkhotel.com
Subway: 23rd Street (6),
14th Street-Union Square (L, N, Q, R, W, 4, 5, 6)

Gramercy introduced a whole new vision to the hotel world. The original Gramercy, opened in 1925, was one of the best addresses in New York, but over the years its luster had palled somewhat – until, with the support of Julian Schnabel, the hotel was transformed into an opulent and colorful artist's studio in 2006. The public spaces are spectacular: black-and-white Moroccan tile floors, 10-foot-tall hand-carved limestone fireplaces, enormous Venetian glass chandeliers. There's a delightful roof-garden restaurant and bar, but the real action is downstairs at the Rose and Jade Bars, home to a stunning collection of contemporary art by Fernando Botero, Andy Warhol, Jean-Michel Basquiat, Damien Hirst, and Julian Schnabel, and furniture designed by Maarten Baas specially created for the hotel.

Price category: $$$$.
Rooms: 185 rooms including 6 suites and a penthouse.
Restaurants: Maialino, Roman trattoria, dinner. **Rose Bar** and **Jade Bar,** midday–4am (reservations required for cocktail bars after 9pm).
History: Designed by Robert T. Lyons and built on the former site of Stanford White's mansion. Humphrey Bogart married his first wife on the roof and the Kennedy family once lived here. Renovated 2006.
X-Factor: Only hotel guests and nearby residents have access to Gramercy Park, New York's only private park, dating from 1831.

Mit dem Gramercy wurde eine neue Hotelvision erfunden. Das ursprünglich 1925 eröffnete Gramercy gehörte zu den ersten Adressen in New York, doch sein Glanz war im Laufe der Jahre verblasst – bis man unter Mitwirkung von Julian Schnabel das Haus 2006 in ein opulent-schönes, farbenfrohes Künstleratelier verwandelte. Vor allem die öffentlichen Räume sind aufsehenerregend: schachbrettartig gemusterte Böden aus marokkanischen Fliesen, drei Meter hohe, handgefertigte Kalksteinkamine und gewaltige Lüster aus venezianischem Glas. Dazu kommt ein wunderbarer Dachgarten mit Restaurant und Bar – doch die größte Attraktion sind die Rose Bar und die Jade Bar, mit einer einzigartigen Kollektion zeitgenössischer Kunst von Fernando Botero, Andy Warhol, Jean-Michel Basquiat, Damien Hirst und Julian Schnabel sowie Möbeln von Maarten Baas, speziell für das Hotel angefertigt.

Le Gramercy, c'est une nouvelle vision de l'hôtellerie. Inauguré en 1925, le Gramercy était l'une des meilleures adresses de New York, mais son éclat s'était terni au cours du temps jusqu'à ce qu'en 2006 on l'ait transformé en un atelier d'artiste excentrique aux couleurs vives avec la collaboration de Julian Schnabel. Les espaces publics sont spectaculaires : sols en carreaux marocains noirs et blancs, cheminées en pierre hautes de trois mètres, énormes lustres vénitiens. Il y a un charmant restaurant bar dans un jardin sur le toit, mais c'est en bas, dans les bars Rose et Jade, que tout se passe : ils accueillent une superbe collection d'œuvres contemporaines signées Fernando Botero, Andy Warhol, Jean-Michel Basquiat, Damien Hirst et Julian Schnabel, ainsi que des meubles créés par Maarten Baas spécialement pour l'hôtel.

Preiskategorie: $$$$.
Zimmer: 185 Zimmer, davon 6 Suiten und ein Penthouse.
Restaurants: Maialino: römische Trattoria, Dinner. **Rose Bar** und **Jade Bar:** 12–4 Uhr (nach 21 Uhr Reservierung dringend erforderlich).
Geschichte: Das Gramercy wurde von Robert T. Lyons entworfen. Humphrey Bogart heiratete auf dem Dach seine erste Frau, und die Kennedys lebten einst hier. Das Haus wurde 2006 renoviert.
X-Faktor: Nur Hotelgäste und Anwohner haben Zugang zum Gramercy Park, New Yorks einzigem Privatpark aus dem Jahre 1831.

Catégorie de prix : $$$$.
Chambres : 185 chambres dont 6 suites et un penthouse.
Restauration : Maialino, trattoria romaine, dîner. **Rose Bar** et **Jade Bar,** de 12h à 4h (réservation nécessaire après 21h).
Histoire : Conçu par Robert T. Lyons et construit par les promoteurs Bing and Bing. Humphrey Bogart s'est marié sur le toit et la famille Kennedy a vécu un moment au second étage. Rénové en 2006.
Le « petit plus » : Seuls les clients de l'hôtel et les riverains ont accès au Gramercy Park, le seul parc privé de Manhattan, créé en 1831.

The Pod Hotel

230 East 51st Street, New York, NY 10022
☎ +1 212 355 0300   ☐ +1 212 755 5029
info@thepodhotel.com
www.thepodhotel.com

Subway: 51st Street (6),
Lexington Avenue/53rd Street (E, V)

Hoteliers Richard Born and Ira Drukier, developers of
Miami Beach's young hipster dormitory, the Townhouse,
opened this New York City version of their concept in 2008.
The Pod has 347 small, minimally furnished rooms, some
with bunk beds, many with shared bathrooms, and a
club-like chill-out rooftop deck, because you don't want to
spend your whole New York City stay hiding in your hotel
room, do you? The big surprise: the Pod's rooms aren't the
sterile cells you'd imagine given the pocket-friendly price
point. Designer Vanessa Guilford (of the Maritime Hotel)
has worked genius with the limited space. The rooms will
remind you of a sailboat berth, with sleek drawers and
clever spaces to stash your belongings in style. The Pod's
most innovative feature, though, is its technology. After
you reserve, you get an email invite to join the hotel's blog.
While in residence you can log in and hook up, online,
with other Pod guests for fun and companionship on that
roof deck, or elsewhere. A new concept indeed: the hotel
as Facebook.

Price category: $.
Rooms: 347 rooms including 5 studios and 2 "Veranda Pods" with
private terraces. 152 of the rooms have shared baths, the rest are
ensuite.
Restaurants: The Pod Café, outdoors, breakfast with pastries from
Balthazar Bakery, beers and snacks after 5pm. **POP@POD,** sports bar
with a full bar, lobster rolls, juicy burgers, foosball tables, open late.
History: The building dates from 1930, and was most recently a
budget hotel called the Pickwick Arms. Completely renovated in
2008, the hotel was re-christened as The Pod.
X-Factor: Cheerful, hip and totally wired.

Die Hoteliers Richard Born und Ira Drukier, Gründer des Townhouse Hotels in Miami Beach, haben diese New Yorker Version ihres Hotelkonzepts 2008 eröffnet. Das Pod bietet 347 kleine, minimalistisch möblierte Zimmer, teils mit Etagenbetten, oft mit Gemeinschaftsbad, und eine klubartige Dachterrasse zum Chillen – schließlich will man sich in New York ja nicht den ganzen Tag im Hotelzimmer verstecken. Dabei sind die Zimmer nicht die sterilen Zellen, die man angesichts der moderaten Preisgestaltung erwarten könnte. Designerin Vanessa Guilford hat hier auf engstem Raum Wunder gewirkt: Dank raffinierter Schubladen und durchdachtem Stauraum kommt man sich vor wie an Bord einer Jacht. Das Highlight des Pod ist allerdings seine innovative Nutzung moderner Technologie. Nach der Reservierung wird man per E-Mail in den Blog des Hotels eingeladen. Im Hotel selbst kann man sich dann einloggen und online mit anderen Gästen verabreden, beispielsweise auf der Dachterrasse. Das Hotel als Facebook – wirklich ein neues Konzept.

Richard Born et Ira Drukier, fondateurs du Townhouse, un hôtel pour jeunes fêtards branchés à Miami Beach, ont inauguré sa version new-yorkaise en 2008. Le Pod compte 347 petites chambres, certaines avec lits superposés, bon nombre avec une salle de bain commune, et une terrasse-lounge sur le toit car on ne vient pas à Manhattan pour rester enfermé. La grosse surprise : compte tenu du prix modeste, les chambres ne sont pas les cellules monacales auxquelles on se serait attendu. Vanessa Guilford (qui a également décoré le Maritime) a fait des miracles dans l'exiguïté. Avec leurs espaces de rangement astucieux et leur mobilier épuré, on se croirait dans un bateau. Mais le plus innovateur, c'est la technologie. Votre réservation faite, vous recevez par courriel une invitation à vous inscrire sur le blog de l'hôtel. Pendant votre séjour, vous pouvez vous connecter, y rencontrer d'autres clients et vous retrouver sur la terrasse, ou ailleurs. Un tout nouveau concept : l'hôtel-Facebook.

Preiskategorie: $.
Zimmer: 347 Zimmer, davon 5 Studios und 2 „Veranda Pods" mit eigener Terrasse. 152 Zimmer haben Gemeinschaftsbäder, der Rest verfügt über ein eigenes Bad.
Restaurants: The Pod Café (auf der Terrasse): Frühstück mit Gebäck aus der Balthazar Bakery; nach 17 Uhr Bier und Snacks. **POD@POD**, Sportbar mit einer großen Getränkeauswahl, Snacks wie Hummersandwiches oder saftigen Burgern, Kickertisch, lange Öffnungszeiten.
Geschichte: Das Gebäude entstand 1930 und war zuletzt eine preiswerte Absteige namens Pickwick Arms. Es wurde 2008 komplett renoviert und als The Pod neu eröffnet.
X-Faktor: Hübsch, hip und komplett vernetzt.

Catégorie de prix : $.
Chambres : 347 chambres dont 5 studios et 2 « Veranda Pods » avec terrasse privée. 152 chambres ont une salle de bain commune, les autres ont une salle de bain attenante.
Restauration : The Pod Café, en terrasse ; petit-déjeuner avec viennoiseries provenant de Balthazar Bakery ; bières et en-cas dès 17h. **POD@POD**, bar sportif avec large choix de boissons, sandwiches au homard, succulents hamburgers, tables de baby-foot, ouvert très tard.
Histoire : Construit en 1930, le bâtiment abritait récemment un hôtel bon marché appelé The Pickwick Arms. Il a été totalement rénové en 2008 et rebaptisé The Pod.
Le « petit plus » : Sympathique, dans le vent et branché.

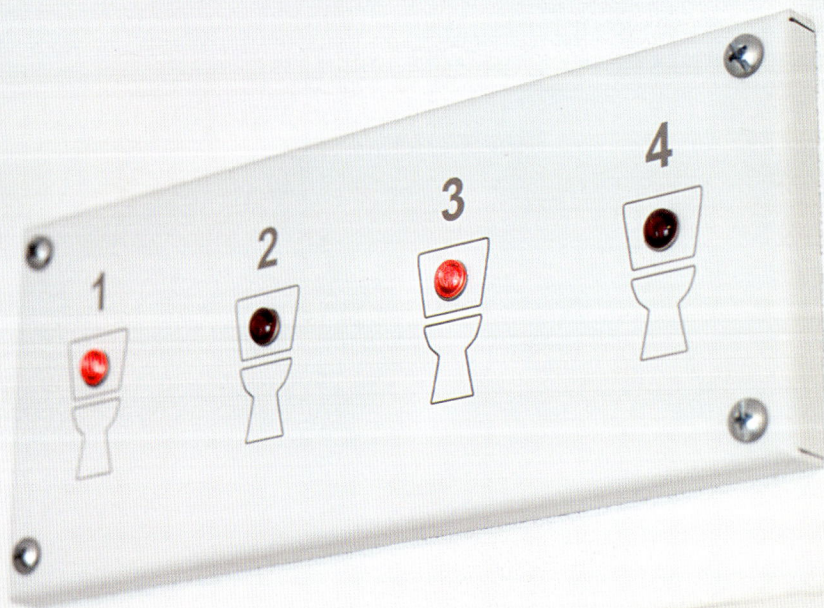

Four Seasons Hotel New York

---

57 East 57th Street, New York, NY 10022
☎ +1 212 758 5700   ☐ +1 212 350 6302
www.fourseasons.com/newyork
Subway: 59th Street (4, 5, 6), 57th Street (F)

This East Side Manhattan hotel is a highlight of the international Four Seasons hotel chain, thanks to architect I.M. Pei, whose spectacular postmodernist structure transforms the old idea of the Grand Hotel into something truly timeless, and modern. Everything about this hotel is impressive, from the sleek limestone facade, to the public spaces with soaring 33-foot lobby ceilings, and the first-class bar. The huge rooms were designed by the firm of Chhada Siembieda, and are decorated in soothing golds and beiges, with creamy English sycamore mouldings and marquetry. While the cost of all this sumptuousness is high, you really get far more for your money here than at other similarly priced hotels in this neighborhood, which is New York's most expensive.

Price category: $$$$.
Rooms: 368 rooms, including 63 suites.
Restaurants: The Garden, regional American cooking, breakfast, lunch, dinner. **Ty Bar,** cocktails and snacks.
History: Newly built and opened in 1993.
X-Factor: Rising nearly 700 feet, with 52 stories this is the tallest hotel building in Manhattan with some of the city's largest guestrooms. TY Warner Penthouse Suite on the 52nd floor at $ 45,000 a night – the most expensive suite in the world.

Dank Architekt I. M. Pei ist das Hotel auf Manhattans East Side ein absolutes Highlight der internationalen Four-Seasons-Hotelkette. Seine spektakuläre postmoderne Konstruktion setzt die alte Idee des Grand Hotel wahrhaft, zeitlos und modern um. Von der glatten Kalksteinfassade bis zu den öffentlichen Räumen wie der zehn Meter hohen Lobby und der erstklassigen Bar ist alles an diesem Hotel imposant. Die großen Gästezimmer in sanften Gold- und Beigetönen mit cremefarbenen Holzeinbauten aus Bergahorn wurden von Chhada Siembieda & Associates gestaltet. Auch wenn all dieser Luxus natürlich seinen Preis hat, bekommt man einiges mehr geboten als in anderen Hotels ähnlicher Preisklasse in dieser Nachbarschaft – immerhin New Yorks teuerstem Pflaster.

Cet hôtel du East Side est un des joyaux de la chaîne Four Seasons. La spectaculaire architecture postmoderniste de I.M. Pei transforme le concept ancien du palace en une expérience résolument contemporaine et atemporelle. Tout y est impressionnant, depuis la façade en pierre calcaire, aux espaces publics, au hall de dix mètres de haut et au superbe bar. Les chambres spacieuses ont été conçues par la firme Chhada Siembieda dans une palette apaisante dorée et beige, avec des moulures et de la marqueterie en sycomore anglais sensuel. Si le prix de cette somptuosité n'est pas donné, vous obtiendrez bien plus pour votre argent que dans n'importe quel autre hôtel de la même gamme de ce quartier, le plus cher de New York.

Preiskategorie: $$$$.
Zimmer: 368 Zimmer, davon 63 Suiten.
Restaurants: The Garden: regionale amerikanische Küche, Frühstück und Lunch. **TY Bar:** Cocktails und Snacks.
Geschichte: 1993 neu erbaut und eröffnet.
X-Faktor: Mit 208 Metern Höhe und 52 Etagen ist das Four Seasons Manhattans höchstes Hotel und bietet gleichzeitig die größten Gästezimmer der Stadt. Das TY Warner Penhouse im 52. Stock ist mit 45 000 $ die teuerste Suite der Welt.

Catégorie de prix : $$$$.
Chambres : 368 chambres dont 63 suites.
Restauration : The Garden, cuisine régionale américaine ; petit-déjeuner déjeuner et dîner. **TY Bar,** cocktails et en-cas.
Histoire : Édifice moderne inauguré en 1993.
Le « petit plus » : Avec ses 208 mètres de hauteur et ses 52 étages, c'est l'hôtel le plus haut de Manhattan. Il compte les chambres les plus spacieuses de la ville. Le 52e étage abrite la suite la plus chère du monde : la TY Warner Penthouse, 45 000 $ la nuit.

Le Parker Meridien

119 West 56th Street, New York, NY 10019
☎ +1 212 245 5000 ☐ +1 212 307 1776
reservations@parkermeridien.com
www.parkermeridien.com

Subway: 57th Street (F, N, Q, R, W)

Who said that a chain hotel has to be bland and corporate? The comfortable, fashionable Le Parker Meridien breaks the mold of the business hotel. It is located in the midtown business district, but its heart is in SoHo – you'll feel that as soon as you step into the classic, minimalist lobby, with its tall columns, and check in at the reservation desk under an enormous hanging work by Damien Hirst. The rooms, designed by Irish-born Colum McCartan (ex-Terence Conran), are modern, understated, with a pleasantly earthy palette of wood-tones, green and orange (book a room above the 24th floor for Central Park views). Walk towards the neon sign in the lobby to find The Burger Joint, where a juicy, classic hamburger and yummy French fries costs less than 10 dollars. And then work it off with a visit to the Meridien's excellent Gravity Fitness Centre, where you'll find a serious, fully equipped gym. It's a great location for both business and pleasure: steps away are most of New York's major corporate offices, 5th Avenue shopping, and Carnegie Hall.

Price category: $$$.
Rooms: 731 rooms, including 100 suites, 200 junior suites.
Restaurants: Norma's, all-day breakfast, lunch. **The Burger Joint,** hamburgers and fries. **Knave,** wine and espresso bar.
History: Built on an empty Midtown site; hotel opened in 1981, renovated in 1998 and 2002.
X-Factor: The outdoor jogging track with Central Park views on the hotel's 42nd floor.

Wer sagt eigentlich, dass Kettenhotels immer öde und ge-sichtslos sein müssen? Das komfortabel-elegante Le Parker Meridien tanzt da aus der Reihe. Es liegt in Midtown, aber sein Herz schlägt in SoHo – was man spürt, sobald man die klassische, minimalistische Lobby mit ihren hohen Säulen betritt und an der Rezeption unter einer gigantischen Arbeit von Damien Hirst eincheckt. Die von Colum McCartan (früher bei Terence Conran) designten Zimmer wirken mit ihrer angenehm erdigen Palette aus Holztönen, Grün und Orange modern und zurückhaltend (oberhalb der 24. Etage genießt man einen Blick auf den Central Park). Die Neonwerbung in der Lobby führt zu The Burger Joint, wo ein saftiger Hamburger mit leckeren Fritten weniger als 10 Dollar kostet. Die Kalorien arbeitet man anschließend im hauseigenen Gravity Gym wieder ab. Mit den wichtigsten New Yorker Unternehmen, den Geschäften der 5th Avenue sowie der Carnegie Hall in Laufweite ist das Meridien idea-ler Ausgangspunkt für Arbeit und Vergnügen.

Qui a dit que les chaînes hôtelières étaient forcément rébar-batives ? Confortable et chic, Le Parker Meridien balaie le cliché de l'hôtel pour hommes d'affaires. Situé à Midtown dans un quartier de bureaux, on se croirait à SoHo dès que l'on s'avance entre les hautes colonnes du hall minimaliste en direction de la réception surplombée d'une œuvre de Damien Hirst. Les chambres décorées par Colum McCartan sont modernes et sobres, dans une apaisante palette de tons ligneux, vert et orange (réservez-en une au-dessus du 24ᵉ étage pour la vue sur Central Park). Dans le hall, suivez l'enseigne au néon du Burger Joint pour savourer un ham-burger saignant et des frites croustillantes pour moins de 10 dollars. Vous pourrez ensuite éliminer les calories dans la salle de gym parfaitement équipée de l'excellent Gravity Spa. L'emplacement est idéal pour les affaires et le plaisir : on est à deux pas du siège des plus grandes sociétés new-yorkaises, des boutiques de 5th Avenue et de Carnegie Hall.

Preiskategorie: $$$.
Zimmer: 731 Zimmer, davon 100 Suiten und 200 Junior-Suiten.
Restaurants: Norma's: ganztägig Frühstück, Lunch. **The Burger Joint:** Hamburger und Fritten. **Knave:** Wein- und Espressobar.
Geschichte: Das auf einem leeren Grundstück in Midtown neu errichtete Haus eröffnete 1981 und wurde 1998 und 2002 renoviert.
X-Faktor: Die Outdoor-Laufbahn auf der 42. Etage mit Blick über den Central Park.

Catégorie de prix : $$$.
Chambres : 731 chambres dont 100 suites et 200 junior suites.
Restauration : Norma's, ouvert toute la journée ; petit-déjeuner et déjeuner. **The Burger Joint,** hamburgers et frites. **Knave,** bar à vins et espressos.
Histoire : Construit sur un ancien terrain vacant de Midtown. Inauguré en 1981, rénové en 1998 et 2002.
Le « petit plus » : Une piste de jogging extérieure au 42ᵉ étage avec vue sur Central Park.

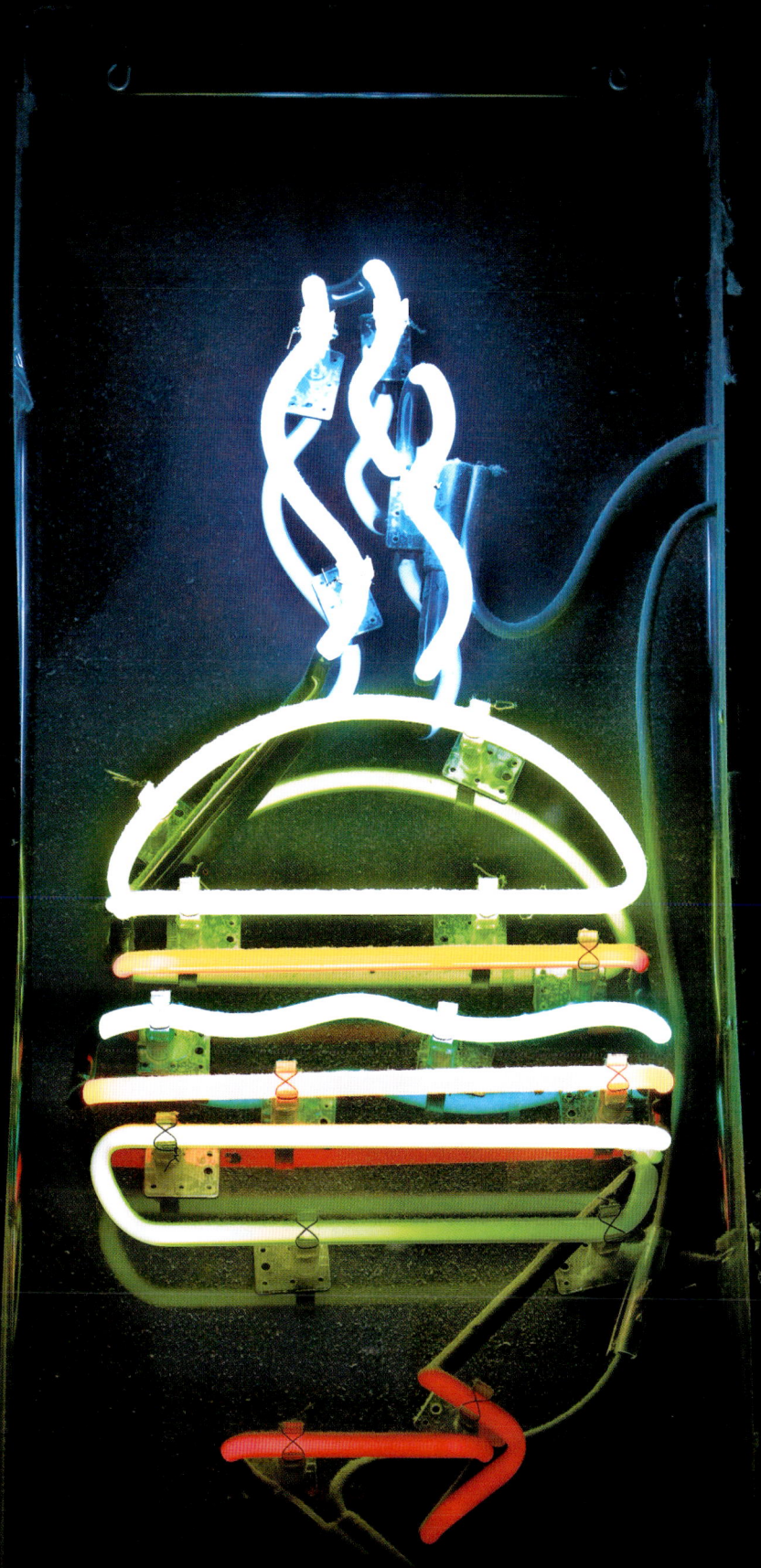

Hudson

356 West 58th Street, New York, NY 10019
☎ +1 212 554 6000   🖷 +1 212 554 6001
www.hudsonhotel.com

Subway: 59th Street-Columbus Circle (1, A, B, C, D),
57th Street (N, Q, R, W)

There is nothing humdrum about the Hudson. Opened in 2000, the hotel was Ian Schrager's first effort at establishing his "hotel-as-lifestyle" concept in New York, and so everything in this Philippe Starck-designed property is extravagant (a giant ceiling mural by painter Francesco Clemente spreads over the Henry Bar like Michelangelo's Sistine Chapel), oversized (the lobby has 40-foot ceilings) and over-the-top (Starck's exaggerated decor includes his signature clashes of Plexiglas and gilt; Louis XV-style chairs and African carved wooden stools). The Hudson is not for people who crave calm; with more than 800 rooms, it's always bustling, and on weekend nights when beautiful young things sip cocktails at the Henry Bar you might be forgiven for thinking you'd accidentally wandered into an Andy Warhol party at the famed 1970s disco Studio 54. If that doesn't suit your mood, you can retreat to the crisp white bedlinens of your tiny, but cozy room, lit by awe-inspiring bedside lamps by British x-ray photographer Nick Veasey.

Price category: $$.
Rooms: 807 rooms, including 13 suites and 2 penthouses.
Restaurants: Hudson Common beer hall and burger joint. **Tequila Park** Mexican fare, outdoor on patio. Cocktails at **Henry** and the **Library Bar.**
History: Hotel opened in 2000. Building constructed in 1928 by the daughter of finance mogul J.P. Morgan as a women's residence. It housed Dutch soldiers in World War II.
X-Factor: The big terraces with deck chairs on the top floors are great for relaxing after shopping and sightseeing.

Das Hudson ist alles andere als alltäglich. Mit dem 2000 eröffneten Hotel versuchte Ian Schrager, sein Konzept des „Hotels als Lifestyle" in New York zu etablieren. Alles an diesem von Philippe Starck designten Hotel ist extravagant (ein riesiges Deckengemälde à la Sixtinische Kapelle von Francesco Clemente ziert die Henry Bar), überdimensional (die Lobby ist zwölf Meter hoch) und abgehoben: Starcks opulentes Dekor bietet Plexiglas und Blattgold, Sessel im Louis-XV-Stil kombiniert mit afrikanischen handgeschnitzten Hockern. Wer Ruhe liebt, ist im Hudson falsch, denn mit mehr als 800 Zimmern ist hier immer etwas los. Und wenn am Wochenende hübsche junge Dinger an der Henry Bar Cocktails schlürfen, kommt man sich vor wie auf einer der legendären Andy-Warhol-Partys der 1970er-Jahre im berühmten Studio 54. Wem das zu viel ist, der kann sich in sein kleines, herrlich gemütliches Zimmer zurückziehen, dessen strahlendweiß bezogenes Bett von ehrfurchtgebietenden Nachttischlampen des britischen Röntgenfotografen Nick Veasey beleuchtet wird.

Au Hudson, rien n'est banal. En l'inaugurant en 2000, Ian Schrager voulait établir à New York le concept d'hôtel « comme style de vie », d'où le fait que tout dans ce lieu conçu par Philippe Stark est grandiose (une fresque de Francesco Clemente orne le plafond du Henry Bar), démesuré (le lobby fait douze mètres de haut sous plafond) et extravagant (le plexiglas côtoie les dorures ; les fauteuils Louis XV, des tabourets africains). Le Hudson n'est pas pour ceux qui aspirent au calme : véritable ruche, les soirs de week-end, quand les beautiful people viennent siroter un cocktail au Henry Bar, on se croirait propulsé dans une fête d'Andy Warhol au Studio 54, la boîte mythique des années 1970. Si vous n'êtes pas d'humeur, vous pouvez vous retrancher entre les draps blancs de votre petite chambre douillette et bouquiner à la lumière de sublimes lampes de chevet signées Nick Veasey, le photographe britannique travaillant avec les rayons X.

Preiskategorie: $$.
Zimmer: 807 Zimmer, 13 Suiten und 2 Penthouses.
Restaurants: Hudson Common Biersaal und Burger-Restaurant. **Tequila Park** mexikanische Küche, draußen auf der Veranda. Cocktails an der **Henry Bar** und der **Library Bar**.
Geschichte: Das 2000 eröffnete Hotel wurde 1928 von der Tochter des Finanzmoguls J. P. Morgan als Frauenwohnheim erbaut und beherbergte im Zweiten Weltkrieg niederländische Soldaten.
X-Faktor: Die Terrassen mit komfortablen Liegestühlen auf den oberen Etagen sind nach Sightseeing-Touren ideal zum Entspannen.

Catégorie de prix : $$.
Chambres : 807 chambres, 13 suites, 2 penthouses.
Restauration : Hudson Common taverne et hamburgers. **Tequila Park** cuisine mexicaine, dehors sur le patio. Cocktails au **Henry** et au **Library Bar**.
Histoire : Hôtel ouvert en 2000. Le bâtiment fut construit en 1928 par la fille de J. P. Morgan comme résidence pour femmes. Pendant la Seconde Guerre mondiale, il a abrité des soldats hollandais.
Le « petit plus » : Les terrasses équipées de transats au dernier étage sont idéales pour se détendre après une journée de shopping.

Mandarin Oriental

80 Columbus Circle at 60th Street, New York, NY 10023
☎ +1 212 805 8800   📄 +1 212 805 8888
monyc-reservations@mohg.com
www.mandarinoriental.com/newyork

Subway: 59th Street-Columbus Circle (1, A, B, C, D)

When Mandarin Oriental opened in 2003, the New York hotel scene got its first taste of Asian contemporary high style – and of an innovative Asian urban design concept. Traditionally, New York hotels are built with the main entrance and lobby at street level. But Mandarin Oriental – like Shanghai's Grand Hyatt – occupies the high floors of a new skyscraper (part of the Time Warner Center built by Skidmore, Owings & Merrill) at the busy Columbus Circle intersection at 60th Street. To check in, you hop on a fast elevator up to the 35th-floor lobby. Upstairs, the mix of Asian and Western decorative arts – glass sculpture by Dale Chihuly, antique Chinese textiles and ceramics – may remind you of your last trip to Hong Kong. Until you glance out the floor-to-ceiling windows to see the park, spread below like your personal green carpet. The rooms are big and plush and come in two color schemes: gold and black, or Chinese red and silver. And this is the Mandarin Oriental, so there's a great spa, too – but just being in this serene aerie of a hotel may be all the relaxation you need.

Price category: $$$$.
Rooms: 244 rooms, including 46 suites.
Restaurants: Asiate, contemporary American cuisine, open for breakfast, lunch, dinner, weekend brunch; **Lobby Lounge,** breakfast, light fare and afternoon tea, 8am–midnight; **MObar,** light fare and cocktails.
History: Built and opened in 2003. Architects Brennan Beer Gorman designed the interiors of the new high rise, which is part of the Time Warner Center complex of shops, performance venues and restaurants.
X-Factor: The best views of any New York hotel.

Das Mandarin Oriental 2003 eröffnete, erhielt die New Yorker Hotelszene einen ersten Vorgeschmack auf den gehobenen modernen asiatischen Stil – und ein innovatives Hotelkonzept. Normalerweise liegen Eingang und Lobby bei New Yorker Hotels im Parterre, das Mandarin belegt aber (wie Shanghais Grand Hyatt) die oberen Etagen des neuen, von Skidmore, Owings & Merrill erbauten Time Warner Center an der Kreuzung Columbus Circle und 60th Street. Zum Einchecken geht es im Expressaufzug auf die 35. Etage. In der Lobby mit westlichem und asiatischem Kunsthandwerk (Glasskulpturen von Dale Chihuly, antike chinesische Textilien und Keramiken) fühlt man sich zunächst wie beim letzten Hongkong-Aufenthalt, bis der Blick aus den deckenhohen Fenstern hinab auf den Central Park fällt und einem den Atem verschlägt. Die Zimmer sind geräumig, elegant und bieten zwei Dekorvarianten in Schwarz und Gold oder Chinesisch-Rot und Silber. Und natürlich gibt es in einem Mandarin Oriental einen großartigen asiatisch inspirierten Wellnessbereich – wenn der Aufenthalt in diesem gelassen-stilvollen Interieur nicht schon Entspannung genug ist.

L'ouverture du Mandarin Oriental en 2003 a donné aux New-Yorkais un avant-goût du chic contemporain et du design urbain novateur d'Asie. À l'instar du Grand Hyatt de Shanghai et contrairement à la plupart des hôtels de Manhattan, qui se trouvent au niveau de la rue, on accède à la réception par un ascenseur qui vous propulse au 35e étage d'un nouveau gratte-ciel (faisant partie du Time Warner Center construit par Skidmore, Owings & Merrill). Le décor, qui mêle arts décoratifs asiatiques et occidentaux (sculptures en verre de Dale Chihuly, céramiques et tissus anciens chinois), vous rappellera peut-être votre dernier séjour à Hong Kong… jusqu'à ce que vous aperceviez par les immenses baies vitrées le tapis vert de Central Park qui s'étend à vos pieds. Les chambres spacieuses et luxueuses sont noires et or, ou argent et rouge de Chine. Le spa est formidable mais le seul fait de baigner dans cette atmosphère sereine et céleste est déjà une garantie de relaxation.

Preiskategorie: $$$$.
Zimmer: 248 Zimmer, davon 46 Suiten.
Restaurants: Asiate: moderne amerikanische Küche, Frühstück, Lunch und Dinner, am Wochenende Brunch. **Lobby Lounge:** Frühstück, leichte Speisen und Nachmittagstee. **MObar:** leichte Speisen und Cocktails.
Geschichte: 2003 erbaut und eröffnet. Die Architekten Brennan Beer Gorman zeichneten für den Innenausbau des Hotelbereichs im neuen Time Warner Center verantwortlich, einem Komplex mit Geschäften, Veranstaltungsräumen und Restaurants.
X-Faktor: Das Hotel mit der besten Aussicht in ganz New York.

Catégorie de prix : $$$$.
Chambres : 248 chambres dont 46 suites.
Restauration : Asiate, cuisine américaine contemporaine ; petit-déjeuner, déjeuner, dîner, brunch le week-end. **Lobby Lounge,** petit-déjeuner, en-cas et collations l'après-midi. **MObar,** en-cas et cocktails.
Histoire : Construit et inauguré en 2003. Les architectes Brennan Beer Gorman ont conçu les intérieurs du gratte-ciel qui fait partie du complexe Time Warner de boutiques et de restaurants.
Le « petit plus » : Les plus belles vues de tous les hôtels de Manhattan.

The Lowell

28 East 63rd Street, New York, NY 10065
☎ +1 212 838 1400   📠 +1 212 319 4230
reservations@lowellhotel.com
www.lowellhotel.com

Subway: 5th Avenue/59th Street (N, R, W),
Lexington Avenue/63rd Street (F)

Life on Manhattan's Upper East Side moves in a more civilized manner than in the rest of the city. Even the noise of the traffic seems muffled by the hush of Old Money. Jackie Onassis lived in this neighborhood, and walking on Madison Avenue, you can picture her, walking amongst the parade of women in vintage Chanel suits and enormous designer sunglasses, to the "three B's" – Bergdorf Goodman, Bloomingdale's and Barneys. Of the handful of venerable hotels in this area, The Lowell is the only one that has managed successfully to update the neighborhood's somewhat stuffy upper-class fuss. Behind its quietly handsome Art Deco facade, the expected hallmarks of old European style (Oriental rugs, overstuffed wing chairs, drapery and sconces) are all there, but the fabrics are bright and new, the palette clean and light. Upstairs, you'll find some of the most intimate and romantic rooms in Manhattan. 33 suites have private fireplaces, 14 have terraces; and they also have fully equipped kitchens with Sub-Zero refrigerator drawers. At The Lowell the tastes of two gilded ages live happily together.

Price category: $$$$.
Rooms: 27 rooms, 47 suites, including one penthouse suite.
Restaurants: The Pembroke Room, breakfast, afternoon tea, pre-theater dinner, evening cocktails, weekend brunch. 24 hour room service. There's a Pet Room Service Menu for dogs and cats. **The Post House,** steak and seafood, lunch and dinner. There's a Pet Room Service Menu for dogs and cats.
History: Designed by Henry Stern Churchill in 1925; restored in 1984. Several suites refashioned by Michael Smith.
X-Factor: Full-size bottles of DDC28 bath products in the marble bathrooms.

Das Leben in Manhattans Upper East Side ist kultivierter als im Rest der Stadt. Selbst der Verkehrslärm scheint vom vornehmen Klang alten Geldes gedämpft. Hier lebte einst Jackie Onassis, und bei einem Spaziergang über die Madison Avenue kann man sie sich gut zwischen der Parade von Frauen in Chanel-Kostümen und riesigen Designer-Sonnenbrillen vorstellen, die zu den „drei Bs" pilgern – Bergdorf Goodman, Bloomingdale's und Barneys. Unter den wenigen ehrwürdigen Hotels dieser Gegend hat es das Lowell als einziges geschafft, den leicht muffigen Oberschicht-Schick zu entstauben. Hinter seiner Art-déco-Fassade finden sich alle Kennzeichen gepflegten europäischen Lebensstils (Orientteppiche, Polstersessel, schwere Vorhänge und Leuchter), doch die Stoffe sind in hellen, modernen Farbtönen gehalten. Die Zimmer zählen zu den behaglichsten in ganz Manhattan: 33 Suiten verfügen über einen offenen Kamin, 14 haben eine eigene Terrasse, und alle bieten eine voll ausgestattete Küche. Im Lowell finden die Geschmäcker zweier Goldener Zeitalter harmonisch zueinander.

La vie dans le Upper East Side se déroule à un pas plus civilisé que dans le reste de la ville. Même le bruit de la circulation semble étouffé par le feutre du vieil argent. Jackie Onassis habitait par ici et on l'imagine parmi le défilé de femmes en tailleur Chanel vintage et énormes lunettes noires griffées remontant Madison Avenue vers les « trois B » : Bergdorf Goodman, Bloomingdale's et Barneys. De la poignée d'hôtels vénérables du coin, The Lowell est le seul à avoir su surmonter le côté légèrement chichiteux et guindé du quartier. Derrière sa belle façade Art Déco, on retrouve les incontournables de la vieille Europe (tapis d'Orient, fauteuils profonds, draperies et lumière tamisée) mais les tissus sont colorés, la palette claire. Les étages abritent les chambres les plus romantiques de Manhattan. 33 suites sont équipées de cheminées, 14 ont des terrasses et des cuisines toutes avec réfrigérateur et congélateur. Ici, les styles de deux âges d'or se côtoient avec bonheur.

Preiskategorie: $$$$.
Zimmer: 27 Zimmer, 47 Suiten, davon eine Penthouse-Suite.
Restaurants: The Pembroke Room: Frühstück, Nachmittagstee, Abendessen vor dem Theaterbesuch, abendliche Cocktails, Brunch am Wochenende, 24 Stunden Zimmerservice. **The Post House:** Steaks, Fisch und Meeresfrüchte, Lunch und Dinner. Für Hunde und Katzen hält der Zimmerservice eine spezielle Tier-Speisekarte bereit.
Geschichte: 1925 von Henry Stern Churchill entworfen, 1984 vollständig saniert. Einige der Suiten wurden von Michael Smith neu gestaltet.
X-Faktor: Marmorbäder mit DDC28-Badeprodukten in normaler Packungsgröße.

Catégorie de prix : $$$$.
Chambres : 23 chambres, 49 suites dont une en penthouse.
Restauration : The Pembroke Room : petit-déjeuner, goûter, dîner avant spectacle, cocktails du soir, brunch les week-ends. Service 24h/24. Le room service propose un menu pour chats et chiens. **The Post House :** viande et fruits de mer ; déjeuner et dîner. Le room service propose un menu pour chiens et chats.
Histoire : Conçu par Henry Stern Churchill en 1924, le bâtiment a été restauré en 1984. Plusieurs suites ont été remaniées par Michael Smith.
Le « petit plus » : Grands flacons de produits de bain DDC28 dans les salles de bain en marbre.

Restaurants

The Empire Diner

Feemans

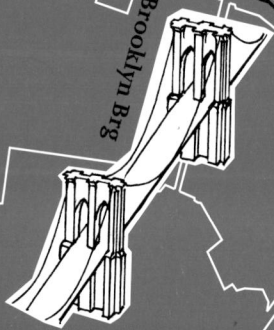

N

Robert F Wagner Jr Park

South Cove

Esplanade

North Cove

Governor Nelson A Rockefeller Park

N End Ave

Tribeca

Greenwich St

Murray St

Warren St

W Broadway

LAIGHT ST

HUDSON ST

Giorgione

CLARKSON ST

7TH AVE S

West Village

Wallsé

The Spotted Pig

La Bergam

Waverly Inn

Mary's Fish Camp

Washington St

Bank St

Perry St

Morton St

Christopher St

W 11th St

W 12th St

W 13th St

W 15th St

W 16th St

Waverly Place

10

VARICK ST

6TH AVE

6TH AVE

Charlie Bird

Blue Ribbon Sushi

Bar Pitti

Joe

W 3rd St

Thompson St

W BROADWAY

Washington Square Park

City B.

W 14TH ST

W 13TH ST

Union Sq Park

Pure Food & W

Irving Pl

CANAL ST

Cipriani Downtov

Omen Azen

SoHo

Bleecker St

Mercer St

BROADWAY

LAFAYETTE ST

3RD AVE

E 14TH ST

E 15th St

Vesey St

Liberty St

Albany St

Bawry Pl

TRINITY PL

CHURCH ST

CHAMBERS ST

Franklin St

N Moore St

Beach St

Duane St

W Broadway

Leonard St

White St

The Odeon

WALKER ST

Greene St

Greene St

Balthazar

Howard St

Spring St

Prince St

Crosby St

Café Gitane

ACME

Nolita

Spring St

Kenmare St

La Esquina

Mulberry St

Mott St

Freemans

Chrystie St

East Village

E 1st St

E 2nd St

E 3rd St

E 4th St

E 5th St

E 6th St

E 7th St

E 8th St

E 9th St

E 10th St

E 11th St

E 12th St

E 13th St

2ND AVE

Stuyves Square

State St

Wall St

Nassau St

William St

Pearl St

ANN ST

PEARL ST

FRANKFORT ST

City Hall Park

Park Row

Thomas Paine Park

Baxter St

Worth St

BOWERY

LAFAYETTE ST

CENTRE ST

Katz's Delicatessen

E HOUSTON ST

Avenue A

Avenue B

Tompkins Square Park

Front St

South St

FRANKLIN D ROOSEVELT DR

Cardinal St

ALLEN ST

Eldridge St

Ludlow St

Essex St

Broome St

Rivington St

Stanton St

Clinton St

Lower East Side

AVENUE C

Avenue D

Brooklyn Brg

Madison St

Cherry St

E River Piers

E BROADWAY

Henry St

Schiller's Liquor Bar

Seward Park

Grand St

Delancey St S

Hamilton Fish Park

Corlears Hook Park

Manhattan Brg

East River Park

Williamsburg Brg

Hudson River Park

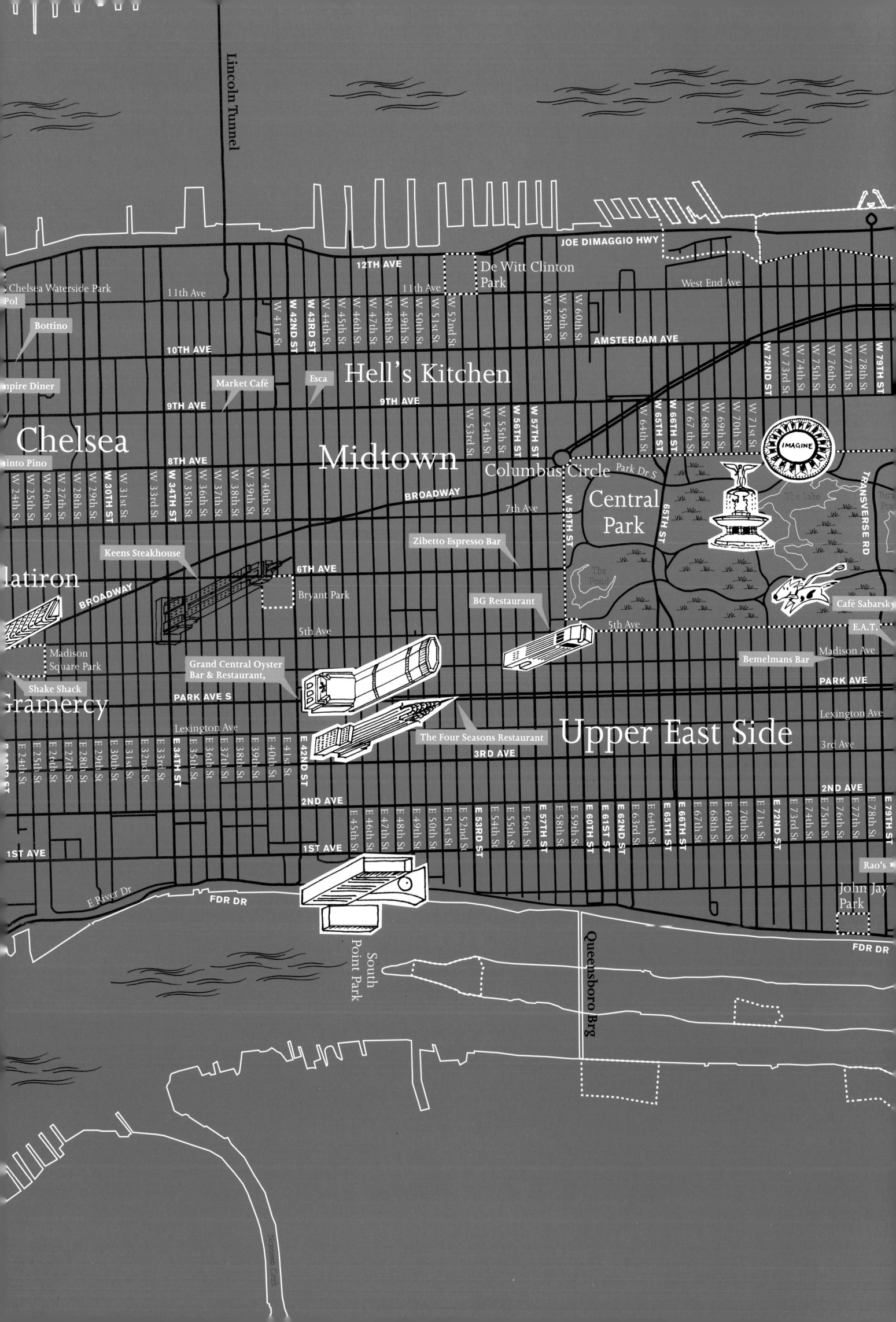

Lincoln Tunnel

JOE DIMAGGIO HWY

12TH AVE

De Witt Clinton Park

11th Ave

Chelsea Waterside Park

Pol

West End Ave

Bottino

W 42ND ST
W 43RD ST
W 44th St
W 45th St
W 46th St
W 47th St
W 48th St
W 49th St
W 50th St
W 51st St
W 52nd St
W 58th St
W 59th St
W 60th St

AMSTERDAM AVE

10TH AVE

W 72ND ST
W 73rd St
W 74th St
W 75th St
W 76th St
W 77th St
W 78th St
W 79TH ST

mpire Diner

Market Café

Esca

Hell's Kitchen

9TH AVE

9TH AVE

W 4 1st St

W 53rd St
W 54th St
W 55th St
W 56TH ST
W 57TH ST

W 65TH ST
W 66TH ST
W 67 St
W 68th St
W 69th St
W 7 1st St

Chelsea

Midtown

IMAGINE

into Pino

8TH AVE

8TH AVE

W 24th St
W 25th St
W 26th St
W 27th St
W 28th St
W 29th St
W 30TH ST
W 31st St
W 33rd St
W 34TH ST
W 35th St
W 36th St
W 37th St
W 38th St
W 39th St
W 40th St

Columbus Circle

Central Park

Park Dr. S

The Lake

BROADWAY

7th Ave

6TH AVE

Zibetto Espresso Bar

W 59TH ST

65TH ST

TRANSVERSE RD

Keens Steakhouse

latiron

BROADWAY

5th Ave

Bryant Park

BG Restaurant

The Pond

5th Ave

Café Sabarsky

E.A.T.

Madison Square Park

Grand Central Oyster Bar & Restaurant,

Bemelmans Bar

Madison Ave

PARK AVE

Shake Shack

PARK AVE S

ramercy

Lexington Ave

The Four Seasons Restaurant

Upper East Side

Lexington Ave

3rd Ave

E 24th St
E 25th St
E 26th St
E 27th St
E 28th St
E 29th St
E 30th St
E 31st St
E 32nd St
E 33rd St
E 34TH ST
E 35th St
E 36th St
E 37th St
E 38th St
E 39th St
E 40th St
E 4 1st St
E 42ND ST

3RD AVE

2ND AVE

E 57TH ST
E 58th St
E 59th St
E 60TH ST
E 61ST ST
E 62ND ST
E 63rd St
E 64th St
E 65TH ST
E 66th St
E 67th St
E 68th St
E 69th St
E 70th St
E 71st St
E 72ND ST
E 73rd St
E 74th St
E 75th St
E 76th St
E 77th St
E 78th St
E 79TH ST

2ND AVE

1ST AVE

1ST AVE

E 45th St
E 46th St
E 47th St
E 48th St
E 49th St
E 50th St
E 51st St
E 52nd St
E 53RD ST
E 54th St
E 55th St
E 56th St

Rao's

E River Dr

FDR DR

John Jay Park

South Point Park

Queensboro Brg

FDR DR

Balthazar

80 Spring Street, New York, NY 10012
☎ +1 212 965 1414
www.balthazarny.com

Subway: Spring Street (6), Prince Street (R, W)

When Balthazar opened in SoHo in 1997, many of its customers wondered if they'd suddenly gotten lost and ended up in the 9th arrondissement. Fabled restaurateur Keith McNally's (also owner of famed Pastis and Schiller's Liquor Bar) bistro manages to be at once picture-perfect Parisian – the tile floor was scuffed and chipped on opening day – and quintessentially New York. You come here to be seen in the most flattering light, sipping Lillet at the long zinc bar, or cutting a deal over moules frites in an oh-so-private booth. Magnifique.

Als das Balthazar 1997 in SoHo eröffnete, fühlten sich viele Kunden umgehend ins 9. Pariser Arrondissement versetzt. Das Bistro des legendären Gastronomen Keith McNally (auch Besitzer des Pastis und der Schiller's Liquor Bar) wirkt authentisch pariserisch – der Fliesenboden war schon zur Eröffnung abgewetzt und gesprungen – und ist zugleich durch und durch New York. Hierher kommt man, um im besten Licht gesehen zu werden, Lillet an der langen Zinkbar zu schlürfen oder bei Moules frites in einem der ach so privaten Separees ein Geschäft abzuschließen. Magnifique.

Quand Balthazar a ouvert à SoHo en 1997, bon nombre de ses clients ont cru avoir soudain atterri dans le 9ᵉ arrondissement. Ce bistrot appartenant à Keith McNally (également propriétaire du fameux Pastis et du Schiller's Liquor Bar) parvient à être parfaitement parisien (le sol carrelé était rayé et ébréché le jour de l'inauguration) tout en étant profondément new-yorkais. On vient s'y faire voir à la lumière flatteuse, siroter du Lillet au long bar en zinc ou négocier un contrat devant des moules frites dans un box intime. C'est Paris sur Hudson !

Interior: A converted warehouse transformed into a replica of a Paris bistro, complete with patina, by Grayling Design.
Open: Mon–Thu 7:30am–midnight (Fri till 1am); Sat 8am–1am (Sun till midnight). Reservations recommended.
Prices: Breakfast $ 4–18; lunch $ 14–33 (duck confit $ 21); dinner $ 21–34.
X-Factor: Come for breakfast to mingle with a dazzling crowd – the pastries and croissants from Balthazar Bakery are superb.

Interieur: Das ehemalige Lager wurde von Grayling Design zur Kopie eines Pariser Bistros umgebaut – mitsamt Patina.
Öffnungszeiten: Mo–Do 7.30–24 Uhr (Fr bis 1 Uhr); Sa 8–1 Uhr (So bis 24 Uhr). Reservierung empfohlen.
Preise: Frühstück 4–18 $; Lunch 14–33 $ (Enten-Confit 21 $); Dinner 21–34 $.
X-Faktor: Das Gebäck und die Croissants der Balthazar Bakery zum Frühstück sind einfach grandios.

Intérieur : Un ancien entrepôt de cuirs transformé en réplique d'un bistrot parisien (patine incluse) par Grayling Design.
Horaires d'ouverture : Lun–Jeu 7h30–24h (Ven jusqu'à 1h); Sam 8h–1h (Dim jusqu'à 24h). Réservation conseillée.
Prix : Petit-déjeuner 4–18 $; déjeuner 14–33 $; dîner 21–34 $.
Le « petit plus » : Petit-déjeuner avec le gratin new-yorkais. Les viennoiseries et les croissants de la Balthazar Bakery sont à tomber !

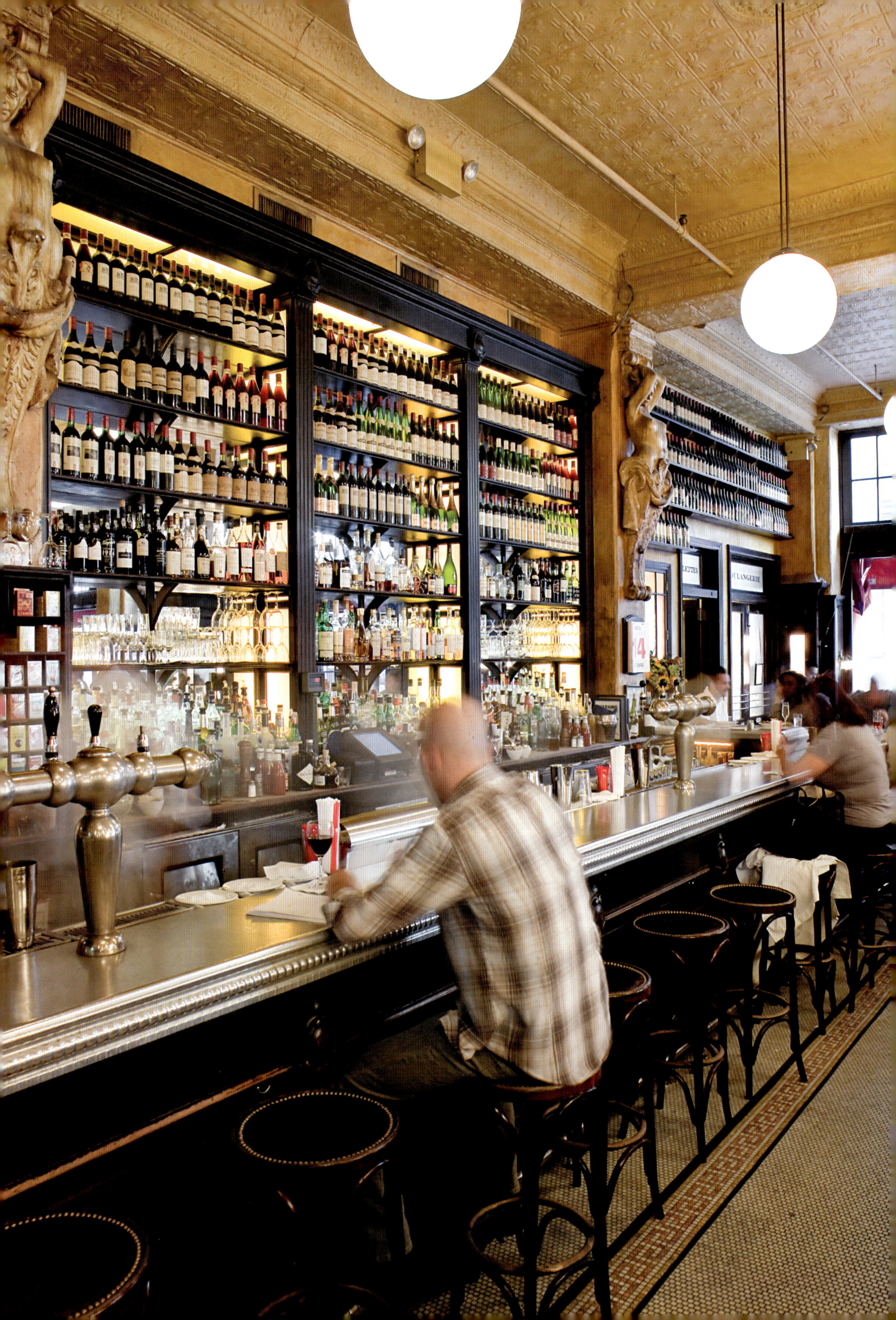

ACME

9 Great Jones Street, New York City, NY 10112
☎ +1 212 203 2121
www.acmenyc.com
Subway: Bleecker Street (4, 6)

The New Nordic Cuisine, or Neo Nordic for short, is regarded by foodies as the greatest innovation since Spain's molecular gastronomy, which is no longer quoted. When Danish chef Mads Refslund opened his restaurant here in early 2012, the New York Times heralded his arrival with the poetic line "Mads Refslund slipped into town in January as quietly as a canoe." He previously worked with René Redzepi in Copenhagen, whose Noma restaurant has already been voted best in the world several times over. The food in Acme is usually served in larger dishes so that more than one diner can share a course. This is known as "family style", not only in Acme, and typifies a wider tendency without the futuristic overtones of sniffing gases or slurping soup out of test tubes; eating together is, by contrast, more fun.

Interior: Former Cajun restaurant. The bistro-style dining area is characterized by warm tones. Bare brickwork, leather corner booths – dive bar style – and conducive lighting.
Open: Sun–Wed 6pm–11pm, Thu–Sat 6pm–midnight, Sat, Sun brunch 11am–3pm.
Prices: Dinner $ 12–38, Selection menu $ 75, á la carte brunch $ 10–22.
X-Factor: A basement bar stays open even after the kitchen closes.

Die Neue Nordische Küche, kurz Neo Nordic, gilt als die Innovation nach der Molekularküche. Als Mats Reflund aus Dänemark hier 2012 sein Restaurant eröffnete, verkündete die New York Times seine Ankunft mit einer poetischen Zeile: Still und heimlich sei er nach Manhatten hineingeglitten, wie in einem Kanu. Reflund hat zuvor bei René Redzepi in Kopenhagen gekocht, dessen Restaurant Noma wurde schon mehrfach zum besten Restaurant der Welt gewählt. Die Gerichte im Acme werden meist in größeren Gefäßen serviert, sodass sich mehrere Esser einen Gang teilen können. Das nennt sich Family Style und bezeichnet einen weiteren Trend, der eben nicht futuristisch erscheint, wie das Einschnüffeln von Gasen oder Suppeschlürfen aus dem Reagenzglas, aber dafür macht das gemeinsame Essen mehr Spaß.

Interieur: Ehemaliges Cajun-Restaurant. Der Gastraum ist als Bistrot in warmen Farben eingerichtet. Offengelegtes Mauerwerk, lederne Sitzecken im Dive Bar Stil, angenehme Beleuchtung.
Öffnungszeiten: So–Mi 18–23 Uhr, Do–Sa 18–24 Uhr, Sa & So Brunch 11–15 Uhr
Preise: Dinner 12–38 $, Degustationsmenü 75 $, Brunch à la carte 10–22 $
X-Faktor: Die Bar im Untergeschoss hat auch nach Küchenschluss noch offen.

La nouvelle cuisine nordique, en abrégé Neo Nordic, est considérée par les gourmets comme la dernière innovation après la cuisine moléculaire d'Espagne qui ne fait plus beaucoup parler d'elle. Lorsque le Danois Mats Reflund a ouvert son restaurant début 2012, le New York Times a annoncé son arrivée en termes poétiques : il se serait glissé, furtivement et secrètement, jusqu'à Manhattan comme dans un canoë. Mats Reflund a travaillé auparavant à Copenhague, chez René Redzepi dont le restaurant Noma a déjà été élu plusieurs fois meilleur restaurant du monde. À l'Acme, les plats sont généralement servis dans de grands récipients pour plusieurs convives. Cela s'appelle, à l'Acme et ailleurs, Family Style et illustre une tendance qui, si elle n'est pas futuriste, rend plus agréables les repas en commun.

Intérieur : Ancien restaurant cajun. La salle est aménagée en bistro aux couleurs chaudes. Maçonnerie apparente, sièges en cuir dans le style Dive Bar, éclairage agréable.
Horaires d'ouverture : Dim-Mer 18h–23h ; Jeu-Sam 18h–24h ; Sam & Dim brunch 11h–15h
Prix : Diner 12–38 $, menu dégustation 75 $, brunch à la carte 10–22 $
Le « petit plus » : Le sous-sol abrite un bar encore ouvert lorsque la cuisine a fermé.

Omen Azen

113 Thompson Street, New York, NY 10012
☎ +1 212 925 8923
Subway: Spring Street (C, E), Prince Street (R, W)

The owner of Omen Azen, Mikio Shinagawa, comes from a most distinguished and cultured old Kyoto family. The family runs Yoshida Sanso, a Kyoto ryokan that was once a princely palace, and Shinagawa's father, Tetsuzan, is a renowned calligrapher. His work (along with Mikio's own) adorns the walls and lanterns of this extraordinarily cultivated Kyoto-style Japanese restaurant that opened in 1981 in the heart of SoHo. The sashimi here is perfection – Shinagawa has the fish flown in daily from Japan for Omen Azen. You'll also find a changing, seasonal menu of dishes and a delicious variety of noodles, as you'd expect in a restaurant named Omen, after its signature kelp and vegetable wheat noodle soup.

Besitzer Mikio Shinagawa entstammt einer alten und angesehenen japanischen Familie, die in Kyoto das Yoshida Sanso betreibt, ein Ryokan in einem ehemaligen Fürstenpalast. Shinagawas Vater Tetsuzan ist ein berühmter Kalligraf – und die Kalligrafien von Vater und Sohn zieren Wände und Lampions dieses außergewöhnlichen japanischen Restaurants im Kyoto-Stil, das 1981 im Herzen SoHos eröffnete. Das Sashimi hier ist schlicht perfekt: Shinagawa lässt den Fisch für das Omen Azen täglich aus Japan einfliegen. Daneben findet man eine saisonal wechselnde Karte sowie ein delikates Angebot von Nudelvariationen – wie die Hausspezialität Omen, eine Weizennudelsuppe mit Seetang und Gemüse.

Le propriétaire d'Omen, Mikio Shinagawa, vient d'une illustre famille de Kyoto où elle gère Yoshida Sanso, un palais princier converti en ryokan. Son père, Tetsuzan, est un célèbre calligraphe dont les œuvres (ainsi que celles de Mikio) ornent les murs et lanternes de ce restaurant japonais au raffinement extrême, ouvert en 1981. Les sashimis y sont parfaits. Shinagawa fait venir le poisson par avion du Japon tous les jours. La carte toujours changeante propose des plats saisonniers ainsi qu'une délicieuse sélection de nouilles, dont la fameuse soupe Omen Azen, aux légumes et varech.

Interior: Japanese country inn style – wooden roof beams, hanging lanterns, fine calligraphy. Designed by owner Mikio Shinagawa, who also designed the Japanese spa in Robert De Niro's Greenwich Hotel.
Open: Mon–Sun 6pm–midnight.
Prices: A la carte dishes $ 15–60; multi-course set dinners $ 68–85.
X-Factor: One of the most authentic Japanese restaurants in Manhattan – a must.

Interieur: Das Design stammt vom Besitzer Mikio Shinagawa, der übrigens auch den Wellnessbereich in Robert De Niros Greenwich Hotel gestaltet hat.
Öffnungszeiten: Mo–So 18–24 Uhr.
Preise: À-la-carte-Gerichte 15–60 $; mehrgängige Menüs 68–85 $.
X-Faktor: Eines der authentischsten japanischen Restaurants Manhattans – ein absolutes Muss.

Intérieur : Mikio Shinagawa, qui a également conçu le spa du Greenwich Hotel de Robert De Niro, l'a aménagé dans le style d'une auberge de campagne japonaise avec poutres apparentes, lanternes et rouleaux de calligraphie.
Horaires d'ouverture : Lun–Dim 18h–24h.
Prix : Plats à la carte 15–60 $; menus 68–85 $.
Le « petit plus » : Un des restaurants japonais les plus authentiques de Manhattan. Un must.

Blue Ribbon Sushi

119 Sullivan Street, New York, NY 10012
☎ +1 212 343 0404
www.blueribbonrestaurants.com
Subway: Spring Street (C, E), Prince Street (N, R, W)

This outpost of the Bromberg Brothers' Blue Ribbon restaurant group (there are branches Uptown and in Park Slope, Brooklyn) has been a smash hit since it opened on this Greenwich Village block in 1995. The name, "Blue Ribbon", is the English translation of "Cordon Bleu", which is where the Bromberg brothers went to culinary school in Paris. The fish is first-rate and reliably fresh every day, and they have lots of inventive sushi rolls that you won't find in any other restaurant. It's a casual place, popular with students from nearby New York University. Be forewarned: they don't take reservations, and the line can often stretch down the street.

Diese Dependance der Blue-Ribbon-Restaurantgruppe der Gebrüder Bromberg ist seit ihrer Eröffnung 1995 in Greenwich Village (weitere Filialen befinden sich in Uptown und am Park Slope, Brooklyn) ein Bombenerfolg. Der Name „Blue Ribbon" – englisch für „Cordon Bleu" – bezieht sich auf die berühmte Kochschule in Paris, in der die Brüder ihre Ausbildung absolvierten. Der hier servierte erstklassige Fisch wird täglich frisch angeliefert und zu innovativen Sushi-Gerichten verarbeitet, die man in keinem anderen Restaurant findet. Dank seiner lockeren Atmosphäre erfreut sich das Blue Ribbon Sushi auch bei den Studenten der nahe gelegenen New York University großer Beliebtheit, was zu langen Warteschlangen führen kann – zumal keine Reservierungen angenommen werden.

Cet avant-poste à Greenwich Village du groupe Blue Ribbon des frères Bromberg (il en existe aussi à Uptown et à Park Slope à Brooklyn) connaît un franc succès depuis son ouverture en 1995. Il tire son nom de l'école « Cordon Bleu » à Paris où les frères ont suivi leur formation culinaire. Le poisson toujours frais du jour est de première qualité et on ne trouve leurs sushis inventifs nulle part ailleurs. L'ambiance décontractée est très prisée des étudiants de la New York University voisine aussi, prenez garde, on ne peut réserver et la queue est parfois longue.

Interior: A small street-level space in a downtown tenement building has been given a contemporary Japanese-rustic inspired re-do (hand carved wood plank booths, bare walls, paper lanterns) by New York Asfour Guzy Architects.
Open: Mon–Sun midday–2am.
Prices: Sushi plate $ 16.50–43.50.
X-Factor: They stay open hours after other restaurants close. So put Blue Ribbon Sushi on your list of late-night dining options!

Interieur: Der kleine, ebenerdige Raum in einem Mietshaus in Downtown wurde vom New Yorker Architekturbüro Asfour Guzy in einem modernen, japanisch-rustikalen Stil gestaltet.
Öffnungszeiten: Mo–So 12–2 Uhr.
Preise: Sushiplatte 16,50–43,50 $.
X-Faktor: Man bekommt hier auch noch etwas zu essen, wenn andere Lokale längst geschlossen haben!

Intérieur : Un petit espace au rez-de-chaussée d'un immeuble d'habitation ayant subi un relookage inspiré façon Japon rustique contemporain par le cabinet New York Asfour Guzy.
Horaires d'ouverture : Lun–Dim 12h–2h.
Prix : Plateau de sushis 16,50–43,50 $.
Le « petit plus » : Les restaurants Blue Ribbon restent ouverts après que les autres établissements ont fermé. C'est donc une bonne adresse pour dîner tard !

Cipriani Downtown

376 West Broadway, New York, NY 10012
☎ +1 212 343 0999
www.cipriani.com
Subway: Spring Street (C, E)

New Yorkers go to some restaurants for the food, but they go to others for the theater. If you are in the mood for a great show, Cipriani Downtown puts on one of the best. Sure, they've got the signature creamy Venetian-style pastas that you'll find at Cipriani's around the world, and their tuna carpaccio with avocado is quite delicious. But what makes this place jump is its clientele of beautiful people, models, and downtown scenemakers. Take a seat – if you can get one – along a banquette, order – of course – a Bellini, and then sit back and enjoy some of the best people-watching in SoHo.

New Yorker besuchen einige Restaurants wegen des guten Essens, andere aber wegen der Show – und wer eine richtig gute Show sehen will, ist bei Cipriani Downtown an der richtigen Adresse! Natürlich gibt es auch hier die hausgemachte venezianische Pasta, für die alle Ciprianis rund um den Globus berühmt sind, und das delikate Thunfisch-Carpaccio mit Avocado. Was diesen Ort aber auszeichnet, ist seine Klientel aus interessanten Menschen, Models und der Downtown-Szene. Wer einen Sitzplatz ergattert, kann sich zurücklehnen, einen Bellini bestellen (was sonst?) und entspannt Leute beobachten – dies ist ein idealer Ort dafür.

À New York, on va dans certains restaurants pour la cuisine, dans d'autres pour le show. Si vous voulez du grand spectacle, le Cipriani Downtown offre l'un des meilleurs. Certes, on y sert les pâtes crémeuses vénitiennes qui font la renommée de la chaîne et leur carpaccio de thon aux avocats est délicieux mais le plus grand attrait du lieu, c'est sa clientèle people. Prenez place de préférence sur une banquette, commandez, naturellement, un Bellini, et savourez l'un des meilleurs défilés de mannequins, de mondains et de célébrités de SoHo.

Interior: High-ceilinged, contemporary Italian bistro designed by Giuseppe Cipriani and Arturo Di Modica. The walls are hung among others with photographs, large and small, by Peter Beard among others.
Open: Midday–midnight, every day. Reservations essential.
Prices: Lunch and dinner entrees $ 26–41.
X-Factor: Try to slip in to the sexy, members-only, private club tucked upstairs.

Interieur: Modernes italienisches Bistro mit hohen Decken, entworfen von Guiseppe Cipriani und Arturo Di Modica. An den Wänden findet man unter anderem Fotografien von Peter Beard.
Öffnungszeiten: Täglich 12–24 Uhr. Reservierung erforderlich.
Preise: Hauptgerichte mittags und abends 26–41 $.
X-Faktor: Wer Glück hat, schafft es bis in den sexy Privatklub im Obergeschoss.

Intérieur : Bistrot italien contemporain, haut de plafond, au décor conçu par Giuseppe Cipriani et Arturo Di Modica. Les murs sont tapissés entre autres, de photos de Peter Beard.
Horaires d'ouverture : De midi à minuit tous les jours. Réservation indispensable.
Prix : Entrées le midi et le soir 26– 41 $.
Le « petit plus » : Essayez de vous glisser dans le séduisant club privé à l'étage.

Giorgione

307 Spring Street, New York, NY 10013
☎ +1 212 352 2269
www.giorgionenyc.com
Subway: Spring Street (C, E)

All you need to know about this absolutely delicious Italian restaurant, located at the far western edge of SoHo and Tribeca, is the co-owner's name: Giorgio Deluca. Yes, it is that Deluca, the legendary co-founder of the Dean & Deluca gourmet grocery chain. In his signature restaurant, the pasta is perfection, the seafood fresh (try the succulent grilled baby octopus), and the service as smooth and smart as the clean white interior. Giorgione's has been a hit with New Yorkers since it opened in 2001, and it draws a lively crowd.

Über dieses hinreißende italienische Restaurant im äußersten Westen von SoHo und Tribeca braucht man nur eines zu wissen, nämlich den Namen des Miteigentümers: Giorgio Deluca … eben jener Giorgio Deluca, der die legendäre Gourmet-Feinkostkette Dean & Deluca mitbegründet hat. Im ersten Restaurant, das ganz allein seinen Namen trägt, sind die Pasta perfekt gekocht, die Meeresfrüchte fangfrisch (versuchen Sie den saftig gegrillten Baby-Oktopus), und der Service ist so makellos wie das ganz in Weiß gehaltene Interieur. Seit der Eröffnung 2001 ist das Giorgione ein Hit bei den New Yorkern und immer gut besucht.

Tout ce qu'il vous faut savoir sur ce restaurant italien absolument délicieux en lisière de SoHo et de Tribeca, c'est le nom de son copropriétaire : Giorgio Deluca, légendaire cofondateur de la chaîne d'épiceries de luxe Dean & Deluca. Les pâtes y sont divines, les fruits de mer d'une fraîcheur impeccable (goûtez le délicieux petit poulpe grillé) et le service aussi lisse et distingué que le décor blanc immaculé. Gorgione fait un tabac auprès des New-Yorkais depuis son ouverture en 2001.

Interior: White, minimal dining area with tan banquettes and industrial steel tables, designed by owner Giorgio Deluca.
Open: Mon–Thu midday–11pm (Fri till midnight; Sat 6 pm–midnight; Sun till 10pm).
Prices: Lunch $ 11–29; dinner $ 19–34.
X-Factor: Giorgione's famous wood-oven pizza is always ranked at the top of the "Best New York Pizza" lists.

Interieur: Weißer, minimalistischer Raum mit beigen Sitzbänken und Edelstahltischen, entworfen von Giorgio Deluca persönlich.
Öffnungszeiten: Mo–Do 12–23 Uhr (Fr bis 24 Uhr; Sa 18–24 Uhr; So bis 22 Uhr).
Preise: Lunch 11–29 $; Dinner 19–34 $.
X-Faktor: Giorgiones berühmte Holzofen-Pizza belegt regelmäßig einen der obersten Plätze auf der „Best New York Pizza"-Liste.

Intérieur : Salle blanche minimaliste avec banquettes brun clair et tables en acier industriel ; conçue par le propriétaire Giorgio Deluca.
Horaires d'ouverture : Lun–Jeu 12h–23h (Ven jusqu'à 24h ; Sam 18h–24h ; Dim jusqu'à 22h).
Prix : Déjeuner 11–29 $; dîner 19–34 $.
Le « petit plus » : Les célèbres pizzas cuites dans un four à bois sont classées n°1 sur la liste des « meilleures pizzas de New York ».

Bar Pitti

---

268 6th Avenue, New York, NY 10014
☎ +1 212 982 3300

Subway: Houston Street (1), West 4th Street (A, C, E, F, V),
West 4th Street-Washington Square (B, D)

Giovanni Tognozzi opened this classic casual Tuscan trattoria in Greenwich Village in 1992, together with the owner of Da Silvano, the famous celebrity Tuscan hangout right next door. The partners split, not so happily, in 2006, but Bar Pitti (the name comes from the Palazzo Pitti, in Florence), under Tognozzi's direction, continues to prosper. Walk by its packed outdoor cafe tables any evening and you'll find supermodels, artists, writers, actors and sports stars galore, from Beyoncé and Donna Karan to Jack Nicholson to New York Mayor Bloomberg. Tognozzi supervises the menu, which includes his famous meatballs, and a rotation of seasonal specials.

Giovanni Tognozzi eröffnete diese klassische toskanische Trattoria in Greenwich Village 1992 zusammen mit dem Eigner des Da Silvano, dem berühmten toskanischen Promi-Restaurant nebenan. Auch wenn sich die Partner 2006 im Streit trennten, floriert die Bar Pitti (nach dem Palazzo Pitti in Florenz benannt) nach wie vor. An jedem beliebigen Abend kann man hier an den dicht besetzten Außentischen Supermodels, Künstler, Schriftsteller, Schauspieler und Sportstars in Hülle und Fülle treffen, von Beyoncé und Donna Karan bis hin zu Jack Nicholson und Bürgermeister Bloomberg. Tognozzi bestimmt die Speisekarte, mitsamt seinen berühmten Fleischbällchen und je nach Saison wechselnden Spezialitäten.

Giovanni Tognozzi a ouvert cette trattoria toscane typique en 1992 avec le propriétaire du Da Silvano, le fameux restaurant toscan très people voisin. Ils se sont fâchés en 2006 mais le Bar Pitti (d'après le Palazzo Pitti à Florence) continue de prospérer. Ses tables en terrasse sont prises d'assaut tous les soirs par des top-modèles, artistes, acteurs, écrivains et vedettes sportives, de Beyoncé et Donna Karan à Jack Nicholson et au maire de New York, Bloomberg. Tognozzi supervise la carte, qui inclut ses fameuses boulettes de viande ainsi qu'une rotation de plats de saison.

Interior: Unpretentious rustic, Tuscan country house: burnt yellow walls hung with vintage sepia photos of 19th century Florence, wood-framed glass doors, bare wood tables.
Open: Mon–Sun noon–midnight.
Prices: Lunch, dinner $ 14–28.
X-Factor: This is one of the best spots in New York to dine alfresco in a sidewalk café atmosphere.

Interieur: Unprätentiös-rustikales toskanisches Landhaus: gelb gestrichene Wände mit vergilbten Florenz-Fotos des 19. Jahrhunderts, holzgerahmte Glastüren und blanke Holztische.
Öffnungszeiten: Mo–So 12–24 Uhr.
Preise: Lunch, Dinner 14–28 $.
X-Faktor: Eines der besten Restaurants der Stadt um in Bistroatmosphäre unter freiem Himmel zu speisen.

Intérieur : Décor toscan rustique sans prétention : murs ocres tapissés de photos sépia de Florence au début du siècle, portes en bois vitrées, tables en bois nu.
Horaires d'ouverture : Lun–Dim 12h–24h.
Prix : Déjeuner, dîner 14–28 $.
Le « petit plus » : Un des meilleurs endroits à New York où dîner en terrasse dans une ambiance de café.

Joe

141 Waverly Place, New York, NY 10014
☎ +1 212 924 6750
www.joenewyork.com

Subway: Christopher Street-Sheridan Square (1),
West 4th Street (A, C, E, F, V),
West 4th Street-Washington Square (B, D)

Although New York City is saturated with Starbucks, the local coffee scene has hit new highs of sophistication in the last few years, thanks to Jonathan and Gabrielle Rubinstein's Joe. All ten branches offer the best coffee and espresso in the city. The one on Waverly Place is especially romantic with a tiny front garden. The beans, roasted locally at Joe's Brooklyn roastery, are organic and fair trade, additionally they also have a compost and recycling program. They also offer limited edition roasts from around the world, hand-brewed to order by impeccably trained baristas. The house special is the caffe latte, which comes topped with a foamy milk and coffee rosetta design.

Obwohl die Straßen in New York City mit Starbucks gepflastert sind, hat die lokale Kaffeeszene in den letzten Jahren qualitativ ganz neue Höhen erreicht – dank Jonathan und Gabrielle Rubinsteins Joe. Alle zehn Filialen bieten den besten Kaffee und Espresso der Stadt, wobei das Café am Waverly Place mit seinem winzigen Vorgarten besonders romantisch wirkt. Die Kaffeesorten stammen aus ökologischem Fair-Trade-Handel und werden in Joes eigener Rösterei in Brooklyn geröstet. Darüber hinaus nimmt Joe The Art of Coffee an einem Kompost- und Recycling-Projekt teil. Außerdem findet man hier limitierte Röstungen aus aller Welt, von erstklassig ausgebildeten Baristas zubereitet. Die Spezialität des Hauses ist der Caffè Latte, serviert mit einer Haube aus geschäumter Milch im Blattmuster.

Dans un New York saturé de Starbucks, les Rubinstein sont parvenus à élever l'art du café à de nouveaux sommets de sophistication. Leurs dix filiales offrent le meilleur de la ville. Celle de Waverly Place est la plus romantique avec sa mini terrasse. Issus du commerce équitable, les grains torréfiés sur place à la torréfaction Joe de Brooklyn sont bios. Joe propose également des éditions limitées de crus du monde entier préparés avec soin par des baristas experts, des pâtisseries de chez Sullivan Street Bakery, PMS Kookie Company et Ceci Cela ainsi que des gâteaux confectionnés par l'humoriste Amy Sedaris. Leur spécialité, le caffe latte, est couronné d'une onctueuse mousse de lait ornée d'un cœur en poudre de café.

Interior: Distressed dark wood floors, exposed brick, designed by Gary Shoemaker Architects.
Open: Mon–Fri 7am–8pm; Sat–Sun 8am–8pm.
Prices: Coffee $ 2–5.
X-Factor: Joe's walls showcase the best barista art from their 170 employees.

Interieur: Verwitterte dunkle Holzböden und unverkleidete Ziegelwände – entworfen von Gary Shoemaker Architects.
Öffnungszeiten: Mo–Fr 7–20 Uhr; Sa–So 8–20 Uhr.
Preise: Kaffee 2–5 $.
X-Faktor: Die einzelnen Filialen zeigen die beste Barista-Kunst ihrer 170 Mitarbeiter an den Wänden.

Intérieur : Conçue par Gary Shoemaker Architects avec de vieux parquets et des briques nues.
Horaires d'ouverture : Lun–Ven 7h–20h ; Sam–Dim 8h–20h.
Prix : Cafés 2–5 $.
Le « petit plus » : Grâce à ses 170 employés, la maison de Joe cultive l'art du café à la perfection.

Mary's Fish Camp

64 Charles Street, New York, NY 10014
☎ +1 646 486 2185
www.marysfishcamp.com

Subway: Christopher Street-Sheridan Square (1),
West 4th Street (A, C, F, V), West 4th-Washington Square (B, D)

Miami-born chef and owner Mary Redding opened this relaxed spot in 2001, as a homage to the roadside fish camps that dot the highways and waterways of Florida. The seafood, flown in every morning from southern waters, is amazingly fresh and delicious, and since Mary is a graduate of the Culinary Institute of America, you can be sure it will arrive perfectly cooked. The West Village location is convenient if you've been shopping or gallery hopping, and it draws a fun crowd. Warning: they don't take reservations, so to be sure of a table, come early or late.

Besitzerin und Köchin Mary Redding aus Miami eröffnete dieses relaxte Restaurant 2001 als Hommage an die vielen „Fish Camps" (Angler-Campingplätze) Floridas. Fisch und Meeresfrüchte werden jeden Morgen aus dem Süden eingeflogen, sind herrlich frisch und erreichen den Tisch perfekt zubereitet – schließlich hat Mary am berühmten Culinary Institute of America gelernt. Die Lage im West Village ist ideal für Shopping- und Galerie-Touren und zieht ein buntes Publikum an. Achtung: Hier werden keine Reservierungen angenommen – wer einen Tisch haben möchte, kommt besser früh oder spät.

Le chef Mary Redding a ouvert ce petit bistrot tranquille en 2001 en hommage aux fish camps qui bordent les routes et les voies d'eau de sa Floride natale. Les fruits de mer acheminés par avion des mers du Sud tous les matins sont frais et délicieux. Mary étant diplômée de la Culinary Institute of America, vous pouvez être sûr qu'ils vous seront servis parfaitement préparés. Le site dans le West Village est pratique quand on fait les boutiques ou le tour des galeries et la clientèle est sympathique. Attention, on ne peut pas réserver ; alors pour être sûr d'avoir une table, venez tôt ou tard.

Interior: The owner designed the no-frills space with butcher-block tables and formica counter, to evoke the style of a typical Florida roadside fish camp.
Open: Mon–Sat midday–3pm; 6pm–11pm.
Prices: Lunch $ 14–24; dinner $17–25.
X-Factor: The grilled whole fish. Mary's offers 4–5 different varieties – Daurade, Florida Pompano, Barramundi – daily.

Interieur: Der Raum wurde von der Besitzerin bewusst schlicht mit einer Resopal-Theke ausgestattet, um den Stil eines Fish Camps in Florida zu imitieren.
Öffnungszeiten: Mo–Sa 12–15 Uhr; 18–23 Uhr.
Preise: Lunch 14–24 $; Dinner 17–25 $.
X-Faktor: Mary's bietet täglich wechselnd 4–5 Variationen von gegrilltem Fisch am Stück, wie z. B. Dorade, Stachelmakrele oder Barramundi.

Intérieur : Pour évoquer le style des petits restaurants de poissons typiques de Floride, la propriétaire a opté pour un décor simple avec des plateaux de tables en billots de boucher et un comptoir en formica.
Horaires d'ouverture : Lun–Sam 12h–15h ; 18h–23h.
Prix : Déjeuner 14–24 $; dîner 17–25 $.
Le « petit plus » : Le poisson entier grillé. Mary en propose tous les jours 4 à 5 variétés (daurade, pompano de Floride, barramundi…).

The Spotted Pig

314 West 11th Street, New York, NY 10014
☎ +1 212 620 0393
www.thespottedpig.com

Subway: 14th Street (A, C, E), 8th Avenue (L),
Christopher Street-Sheridan Square (1)

This West Village restaurant opened in 2004 to rave reviews, and introduced New Yorkers to a new cuisine: British gastro-pub. Chef and co-owner April Bloomfield is from Birmingham, England, and she trained at London's River Café and at Alice Waters' Chez Panisse in Berkeley, the birthplace of California cuisine. Her food, made with the freshest local ingredients whenever possible, is at once folksy and chic – you can get everything from sauteed quail to a pot of pickles. This is one of artist Elizabeth Peyton's favorite restaurants, and she's not the only fan – at peak hours, the line to get a table has been known to stretch down the block.

The Spotted Pig eröffnete 2004 im West Village unter begeistertem Applaus der Kritiker und führte die britische Gastro-Pub-Küche in New York ein. Küchenchefin und Mitbesitzerin April Bloomfield stammt aus dem englischen Birmingham und lernte im Londoner River Café und später bei Alice Waters im Chez Panisse in Berkeley, dem Geburtsort der California-Cuisine. Die Speisen werden aus frischen Zutaten der Region zubereitet, und die Karte bietet Ausgefallenes neben Traditionellem – von der sautierten Wachtel bis zur Schale Mixed Pickles. Die Malerin Elizabeth Peyton zählt das Spotted Pig zu einem ihrer Lieblingsrestaurants – und steht damit nicht allein: Zu Stoßzeiten geht die Schlange der Wartenden schon mal um den Block.

Salué par les critiques à son ouverture en 2004, ce restaurant a fait découvrir aux New-Yorkais une nouvelle cuisine : la gastronomie de pub britannique. L'anglaise April Bloomfield, chef et copropriétaire du lieu, s'est formé au River Café à Londres puis au Chez Panisse d'Alice Waters à Berkeley, berceau de la cuisine californienne. Ses plats, à la fois simples et chic, sont préparés avec les ingrédients locaux les plus frais, qu'il s'agisse de cailles sautées ou de pickles. C'est une des adresses préférées d'Elizabeth Peyton et elle n'est pas la seule : la queue s'étire parfois jusqu'au coin de la rue.

Interior: Wood plank floors and walls, pig memorabilia, mis-matched fabrics and furniture. Designed by co-owner Ken Friedman.
Open: Mon–Sun midday–2am (Sat, Sun brunch from 11am).
Prices: Lunch $ 15–18; dinner $ 18–33. Char-grilled Burger with Roquefort Cheese $ 15; Prosciutto and Ricotta Tart $ 16.
X-Factor: The bar has an excellent selection of British-style hand-pulled ales.

Interieur: Holzdielenboden, holzvertäfelte Wände, Schweine-Nippes, zusammengewürfelte Möbel und Bezüge. Entworfen von Mitbesitzer Ken Friedman.
Öffnungszeiten: Mo–So 12–2 Uhr (Sa, So Brunch ab 11 Uhr).
Preise: Lunch 15–18 $; Dinner 18–33 $. Burger vom Holzkohlengrill mit Roquefort 15 $, Prosciutto und Ricotta-Tarte 16 $.
X-Faktor: Die Bar bietet eine hervorragende Auswahl an britischen Fassbieren.

Intérieur : Parquet et boiseries, collection de petits cochons, tissus et meubles dépareillés. Décoré par le copropriétaire Ken Friedman.
Horaires d'ouverture : Lun–Dim 12h–2h (Sam, Dim brunch à partir de 11h).
Prix : Déjeuner 15–18 $; dîner 18–33 $. Hamburger grillé au charbon avec Roquefort 15 $; tarte au prosciutto et ricotta 16 $.
Le « petit plus » : Une excellente sélection de bières anglaises à la pression.

Wallsé

344 West 11th Street, New York, NY 10014
☏ +1 212 352 2300
www.kg-ny.com

Subway: 8th Avenue (L), 14th Street (A, C, E),
Christopher Street-Sheridan Square (1)

Wallsé is a restaurant for all the senses. This comfortable West Village Viennese spot, opened in 2000, serves fine cuisine, fine art and modern Viennese design all at once. Julian Schnabel is a regular here, and the walls are hung with selections from his personal art collection including his portrait of Wallsé's owner, Austrian chef Kurt Gutenbrunner (who also owns Blaue Gans in Tribeca and Café Sabarsky at Neue Galerie). There are also works by Albert Oehlen, Martin Kippenberger and Easy Rider actor Dennis Hopper. The haute contemporary Viennese main dishes and the superb strudel will make your aesthetic delight complete.

Das Wallsé ist ein Restaurant, das alle Sinne anspricht: 2000 eröffnet, bietet dieses gemütliche Stückchen Wien in West Village eine exzellente Küche, exquisite Kunst und modernes Wiener Design. Der Maler und Filmregisseur Julian Schnabel zählt zu den Stammgästen des Wallsé, an dessen Wänden eine Auswahl seiner privaten Kunstsammlung hängt, darunter auch ein Porträt des österreichischen Besitzers und Kochs Kurt Gutenbrunner (der auch die Blaue Gans in Tribeca und das Café Sabarsky in der Neuen Galerie betreibt). Neben diesen Werken findet man hier aber auch Arbeiten von Albert Oehlen, Martin Kippenberger und Easy-Rider-Star Dennis Hopper – ein ästhetischer Genuss, der durch die gehobene Wiener Küche und den fantastischen Strudel noch abgerundet wird.

Wallsé est un restaurant pour tous les sens. On y sert de la grande cuisine contemporaine, de l'art et du design autrichiens. Julian Schnabel est un habitué et les murs sont tapissés d'un choix de sa collection privée dont un portrait du propriétaire, le chef autrichien Kurt Gutenbrunner (qui possède aussi le Blaue Gans à Tribeca et le Café Sabarsky de la Neue Galerie). On y voit également des œuvres d'Albert Oehlen, de Martin Kippenberger et de Dennis Hopper. Les délicieux plats principaux et le divin strudel achèveront de combler votre expérience esthétique.

Interior: Austere, early 20th century modern Viennese; design by Constantin Wickenburg Architects, original chairs from Thonet Vienna designed by Adolf Loos.
Open: Dinner Mon–Sun 5:30pm–11pm; brunch Sat–Sun 11am–2:15pm; lunch Sun 11:30am–2:30p.m.
Prices: Dinner $ 26–38; brunch $ 11–26.
X-Factor: The restaurant is named after the Austrian birthplace of the owner.

Interieur: Design von Constantin Wickenburg Architects im Wiener Stil des frühen 20. Jahrhunderts, mit original erhaltenen Thonetstühlen von Adolf Loos.
Öffnungszeiten: Dinner Mo–So 17.30–23 Uhr; Brunch Sa–So 11–14.15 Uhr.
Preise: Dinner 26–38 $; Brunch 11–26 $.
X-Faktor: Das Restaurant wurde nach dem Geburtsort des österreichischen Eigners benannt.

Intérieur : Décor viennois austère du début du 20ᵉ siècle, conçu par la firme Constantin Wickenburg. Chaises Thonet viennoises originales dessinées par Adolf Loos.
Horaires d'ouverture : Dîner Lun–Dim 17h30–23h ; brunch Sam–Dim 11h–14h15.
Prix : Dîner 26–38 $; brunch 11–26 $.
Le « petit plus » : Le restaurant porte le nom du village autrichien au bord du Danube, datant du 15ᵉ siècle, où est né le propriétaire.

Waverly Inn

16 Bank Street, New York, NY 10014
☎ +1 917 828 1154
Subway: 14th Street (A, C, E, 1, 2, 3), 8th Avenue (L)

Graydon Carter, editor of Vanity Fair, took over this Greenwich Village icon with Sean MacPherson and Eric Goode (also creators of The Maritime and Bowery Hotels) in 2006. They have transformed the old "Ye Waverly Inn" into a New York version of London's Groucho Club, a hangout for the city's best and brightest. There is an air of exclusivity about the restaurant yet the menu consists of basic comfort food (steaks, pot pie, mac & cheese). But cuisine isn't why everyone wants a seat in Waverly's clubby main dining room with its red leather banquettes and low amber lighting. You come for the stars: Robert De Niro and Gwyneth Paltrow, Sting, Calvin Klein and Donna Karan.

Graydon Carter, der Herausgeber der Vanity Fair, übernahm diese Ikone des Greenwich Village 2006 zusammen mit Sean MacPherson und Eric Goode (Schöpfer des Maritime und des Bowery Hotel) und verwandelte das alte „Ye Waverly Inn" in die New Yorker Version des Londoner Groucho Club, Treffpunkt der Schönen und Reichen. Das Restaurant umgibt ein Hauch der Exklusivität, doch die Karte bietet schlichtes Comfort Food (Steaks, Pasteten, Makkaroni & Käse), aber das Publikum kommt auch nicht wegen der Küche in das Lokal mit den roten Lederbänken – man kommt wegen der Stars wie Robert De Niro, Gwyneth Paltrow, Sting, Calvin Klein und Donna Karan.

Graydon Carter, rédacteur en chef de Vanity Fair, Sean MacPherson et Eric Goode se sont emparés de ce haut lieu de Greenwich Village en 2006 et l'ont transformé en version new-yorkaise du Groucho Club de Londres, le repaire de la crème de la crème. Il y règne une atmosphère exclusive, la carte propose cependant des plats basiques (steaks, tourtes, gratin de macaronis). Toutefois, on ne s'arrache pas une table dans la salle à manger aux banquettes en cuir rouge et à l'éclairage ambré pour la cuisine mais pour les stars : De Niro, Gwyneth Paltrow, Sting, Calvin Klein et Donna Karan.

Interior: Located in a landmark 19th-century townhouse. The murals that depict famous characters are by Vanity Fair illustrator Edward Sorel.
Open: Sun–Thu 6pm–11:45pm (Fri–Sat till 12:45am). Reservations accepted 2 weeks in advance.
Prices: Dinner $ 21–51.
X-Factor: Make sure to get a table in the main dining room, not in the glass conservatory, which is considered to be "Siberia".

Interieur: Stadthaus aus dem 19. Jahrhundert. Die Wandmalereien stammen vom Vanity-Fair-Illustrator Edward Sorel.
Öffnungszeiten: So–Do 18–23.45 Uhr (Fr, Sa bis 0.45 Uhr). Reservierungen müssen 2 Wochen im Voraus vorgenommen werden.
Preise: Dinner 21–51 $.
X-Faktor: Reservieren Sie einen Tisch im Restaurant selbst – und nicht etwa im Wintergarten, der als „Sibirien" gilt.

Intérieur : Situé dans une maison du 19ᵉ siècle. L'illustrateur de Vanity Fair, Edward Sorel, a réalisé les fresques des célébrités.
Horaires d'ouverture : Dim–Jeu 18h–23h45 (Ven, Sam jusqu'à 0h45). Réservations acceptées deux semaines à l'avance.
Prix : Dîner 21–51 $.
Le « petit plus » : Assurez-vous de ne pas être dans le jardin d'hiver, baptisé « la Sibérie » par les habitués.

American Naval Heroes

SPANISH

AMERICAN

WAR

Santiago—Cuba
July 3rd 1898.

WAR

La Bergamote

177 9th Avenue, New York, NY 10011
☎ +1 212 627 9010
www.labergamotenyc.com
Subway: 23rd Street (C, E)

Temptation is everywhere at this authentic French patisserie in Chelsea. Flaky almond croissants, crusty fragrant baguettes, tartes tatin and pillowy, multi-layered Napoleons sing out to customers from inside a gleaming glass case. Opened in 1998 by two Frenchmen from Nancy, Stephan Willemin and Romain Lamaze, La Bergamote quickly became one of the city's leading French bakeries. You can order a café au lait and eat an éclair at one of the tiny tables, or just grab a quick take-out lunch that is, nevertheless, elegant – try their tasty baguette sandwiches or some Quiche Lorraine.

Diese original französische Patisserie mitten in Chelsea ist eine einzige Versuchung: Croissants mit Mandeln, knusprige, duftende Baguettes, Tartes Tatin und luftige, mehrschichtige Napoleons in glänzenden Glasvitrinen ziehen die Kundschaft magisch an. 1998 von Stephan Willemin und Romain Lamaze aus Nancy eröffnet, entwickelte sich La Bergamote schnell zu einer der führenden französischen Feinbäckereien der Stadt. Man kann an einem der winzigen Tische sein Eclair essen und einen Café au Lait dazu trinken oder einfach einen schnellen Lunch zum Mitnehmen ordern und bekommt immer etwas Exquisites – versuchen Sie einmal die Baguette-Sandwiches oder die Quiche Lorraine.

Dans cette authentique pâtisserie française, la tentation est partout. De derrière leurs vitrines étincelantes, les croissants aux amandes, les baguettes croustillantes, les tartes tatins et les voluptueux napoléons vous font les yeux doux. Ouverte en 1998 par deux Nancéens, Stephan Willemin et Romain Lamaze, La Bergamote est vite devenue l'une des pâtisseries préférées des New-Yorkais. On peut commander un café au lait et déguster un éclair à l'une des minuscules tables ou emporter une élégante barquette-repas. Essayez leur délicieux sandwichs baguettes ou une quiche lorraine.

Interior: Modern French patisserie with glass cases and Art Nouveau inspired murals, designed by owners Willemin and Lamaze.
Open: Mon–Wed 7am–8pm (Thu–Sat till 10pm, Sun till 9pm).
Prices: Pastries, quiches $ 4–14.
X-Factor: This is the home of some of the finest French desserts in the city; be sure to try the "Bergamotier", made of bergamot mousse, chocolate and caramel ganache.

Interieur: Moderne französische Patisserie mit Glasvitrinen. Die Wandmalereien im Stil des Art nouveau wurden von den Besitzern Willemin und Lamaze entworfen.
Öffnungszeiten: Mo–Mi 7–20 Uhr (Do–Sa bis 22 Uhr, So bis 21 Uhr).
Preise: Feingebäck, Quiches 4–14 $.
X-Faktor: Hier findet man eine der köstlichsten französischen Nachspeisen in New York – die „Bergamotier" aus Bergamotte-Mousse, Schokolade und Karamellganache.

Intérieur : Pâtisserie avec des fresques d'inspiration Art Nouveau. Conçue par les propriétaires Willemin et Lamaze.
Horaires d'ouverture : Lun–Mer 7h–20h (Jeu–Sam jusqu'à 22h, Dim jusqu'à 21h).
Prix : Pâtisseries, quiches 4–14 $.
Le « petit plus » : Vous y trouverez certains des meilleurs desserts français de la ville. Goûtez absolument le « Bergamotier » : mousse de bergamote, chocolat et ganache au caramel.

Tía Pol

205 10th Avenue, New York, NY 10011
☎ +1 212 675 8805
www.tiapol.com
Subway: 23rd Street (C, E)

The bar at Tía Pol is usually elbow-to-elbow with lively people, for good reason. Although this tiny West Chelsea tapas bar, opened in 2004, has American owners, the place is like a piece of Spain re-planted in Manhattan. Even the basic dishes seem special here. Make sure to order the ensalada de alcachofa (crispy artichoke and white asparagus salad with lemon vinaigrette) or satisfy your sweet tooth with an order of leche frita (Basque fried custard). Delicious, fun, and best of all, affordable.

An der Bar des Tía Pol geht es eng und lebhaft zu, und das aus gutem Grund. Obwohl die 2004 eröffnete, winzige Tapas-Bar in West Chelsea amerikanische Besitzer hat, ist sie wie ein Stück Spanien inmitten Manhattans. Sogar ganz einfache Dinge, schmecken hier besonders gut. Bestellen Sie auf jeden Fall die ensalada de alcachofa (knackiger Salat aus Artischocken und weißem Spargel mit Zitronen-Vinaigrette), oder tun Sie Ihrer inneren Naschkatze etwas Gutes mit einer Portion leche frita (überbackener Milchschaum). Lecker, ausgefallen und vor allem erschwinglich.

Tía Pol est généralement bondé et animé, à juste titre. Ce minuscule bar à tapas ouvert en 2004 a beau appartenir à des Américains, on croirait un petit morceau d'Espagne implanté à Manhattan. Même les basiques sont teintés d'originalité. Il faut absolument goûter à l'ensalada de alcachofa (salade d'artichauts croquants et d'asperges blanches accompagnée d'une sauce vinaigrette au citron) ou céder à la tentation d'une leche frita (dessert sucré du pays basque). Délicieux, sympathique et, en plus, abordable !

Interior: Traditional-style tapas bar; designed by owner Heather Belz.
Open: Mon 5:30pm–11pm; Tue–Thu midday–11pm (Fri till midnight); Sat 11am–midnight (Sun till 10:30pm).
Prices: Tapas $ 4–29.
X-Factor: Come here to eat Spanish tapas that are even better than in Spain.

Interieur: Gemütliche, traditionell gehaltene Tapas-Bar, gestaltet von der Besitzerin Heather Belz.
Öffnungszeiten: Mo 17.30–23 Uhr; Di–Do 12–23 Uhr (Fr bis 24 Uhr); Sa 11–24 Uhr (So bis 22.30 Uhr).
Preise: Tapas 4–29 $.
X-Faktor: Die spanischen Tapas sind hier noch besser als in Spanien.

Intérieur : Bar à tapas traditionnel décoré par la propriétaire Heather Belz.
Horaires d'ouverture : Lun 17h30–23h ; Mar–Jeu 12h–23h (Ven jusqu'à 24h) ; Sam 11–24h (Dim jusqu'à 22h30).
Prix : Tapas de 4–29 $.
Le « petit plus » : Venez y déguster des tapas espagnoles meilleures qu'en Espagne.

Bar Menu
3–5

- patatas bravas
- garbanzos fritos
- chorizo al jerez
- almendras y aceitunas
- tortilla española

- croquetas de jamon
  croquettes del dia
- lomo a bordelesa
- gildas
- salpicon
- pan tomat

- ibericos

Bottino

246 10th Avenue, New York, NY 10001
☎ +1 212 206 6766
www.bottinonyc.com
Subway: 23rd Street (C, E)

Bottino is a terrific place to stop for lunch or dinner after you've worked your way through a few dozen of West Chelsea's more than 100 art galleries. Opened in 1998, it draws an interesting crowd from the fashion and art worlds. The atmosphere is relaxed and convivial, whether you are sitting inside at a round dining table on an wooden Eames chair, or in the lovely garden with its white Bertoia chairs. The hearty Tuscan dishes are delicious (entrees include Orecchiette with broccoli rabe and boar sausage), the lighting is gentle and the walls are bare – a relaxing change from all that art you've just been taking in.

Wenn man sich durch mehrere Dutzend der über 100 Galerien in West Chelsea gekämpft hat, ist das Bottino der ideale Ort für ein Mittag- oder Abendessen. In dem 1998 eröffneten Restaurant trifft sich ein buntes Publikum aus Kunst- und Modewelt. Die Atmosphäre ist sowohl drinnen an den runden Tischen mit Eames-Stühlen als auch im wunderbaren Garten mit weißen Bertoia-Stühlen entspannt-gesellig. Die herzhafte toskanische Küche (z. B. Orecchiette mit Brokkoli und Wildschweinwurst), die gedämpfte Beleuchtung und die schmucklosen Wände bieten eine erholsame Abwechslung nach all den überladenen Galerien.

Bottino est un lieu épatant où se reposer après avoir fait le tour des quelques cent galeries de West Chelsea. Ouvert en 1998, il attire une clientèle venue du monde de la mode et des arts. L'ambiance y est détendue et conviviale, que vous soyez assis à l'intérieur autour d'une table ronde sur une chaise Eames en bois, ou dans le charmant jardin avec ses sièges Bertoia blancs. Les plats toscans sont copieux et délicieux (les entrées incluent des orecchiette aux brocolis et des saucisses de sanglier), l'éclairage est doux et les murs nus, de quoi reposer vos yeux fatigués par tant d'art.

Interior: 100-year-old hardware store, transformed into an eclectic mix of mid-century modern design by Thomas Leeser.
Open: Tue–Sat midday–3:30pm; Mon–Sat 6pm–11:30pm (Sun till 10:30pm).
Prices: Lunch $ 12–22; dinner $ 16–30;
X-Factor: In the colder months, a white tent is erected over the wonderful garden, so you can still enjoy al fresco dining.

Interieur: 100 Jahre alter Eisenwarenhandel, von Thomas Leeser mit einer Mischung aus 1950er-Designobjekten gestaltet.
Öffnungszeiten: Di–Sa 12–15.30 Uhr; Mo–Sa 18–23.30 Uhr (So bis 22.30 Uhr).
Preise: Lunch 12–22 $; Dinner 16–30 $;
X-Faktor: Während der kalten Monate wird in dem Innenhofgarten ein weißes Zelt errichtet, sodass man dort trotzdem speisen kann.

Intérieur : Ancienne quincaillerie centenaire aménagée avec un mobilier design éclectique des années 1950 par Thomas Leeser.
Horaires d'ouverture : Mar–Sam 12h–15h30 ; Lun–Sam 18h–23h30 (Dim jusqu' à 22h30).
Prix : Déjeuner 12–22 $; dîner 16–30 $;
Le « petit plus » : L'hiver, une tente blanche dressée dans le ravissant jardin permet de dîner à l'extérieur.

El Quinto Pino

401 West 24th Street, New York, NY 10011
☎ +1 212 206 6900
www.elquintopinonyc.com
Subway: 23rd Street (C, E)

This terrific tapas bar opened in 2007. Owned and operated by its original chef, Alexandra Raij, and her husband, Eder Montero, El Quinto Pino is the multi-regional cousin of Txikito, their Basque restaurant across the street. There are no tables, and only 16 stools, so the atmosphere is really authentically Madrid. The adventurous food includes the traditional Spanish tapas dishes, but also some unusual inventions that add flavors from Asia, like ginger and mustard oil, to the mix. This is the place to drop in after a gallery crawl through Chelsea, to begin the evening with conversation, olives and cheese, and a glass of Spanish wine.

Die fantastische Bar wurde 2007 eröffnet. Besitzer der Bar sind die Küchenchefin Alexandra Raij und ihr Mann Eder Montero, die auch das baskische Restaurant Txikito gegenüber betreiben. Das El Quinto Pino ist nur eine Bar – es gibt keine Tische und nur 16 Barhocker, ganz als wäre man in Madrid. Das innovative Angebot umfasst traditionelle spanische Tapas, aber auch ungewöhnliche Kreationen, die die Aromen Asiens, wie Ingwer und Senföl, ins Spiel bringen. Dies ist der perfekte Ort, um nach einer Tour durch die Galerien Chelseas zu entspannen und den Abend mit Gesprächen, Oliven, Käse und einem Glas spanischen Wein einzuläuten.

Un formidable bar à tapas ouvert en 2007. Alexandra Raij, cuisinière en Chef dès le début, et son mari Eder Montero, en sont les propriétaires et le dirigent. El Quinto Pino est le cousin régional du Txikito, le restaurant basque situé de l'autre côté de la rue, à la différence qu'il s'agit vraiment d'un bar (il n'y a pas de tables, juste 16 tabourets) et qu'on se croirait à Madrid. La carte inclut les tapas traditionnelles mais également quelques créations originales, ajoutant un parfum asiatique comme l'huile au gingembre et à la moutarde. C'est l'endroit idéal où s'arrêter après avoir fait les galeries de Chelsea et entamer la soirée avec une conversation, des olives, du fromage et un verre de vin espagnol.

Interior: The beautiful small room with high ceilings, distressed mirrors and sensuously curved white marble bar was designed by Berman Horn Studio.
Open: Mon–Thu 5pm–midnight (Fri, Sat till 1am, Sun till 11pm). No reservations accepted.
Prices: Tapas $ 5–14.
X-Factor: Make sure to try the house special, an absolutely scrumptious sea urchin panini.

Interieur: Der schöne kleine Raum mit den hohen Decken, den matten Spiegeln und der sinnlich geschwungenen weißen Marmorbar wurde von Berman Horn Studio gestaltet.
Öffnungszeiten: Mo–Do 17–24 Uhr (Fr, Sa bis 1, So bis 23 Uhr). Keine Reservierungen.
Preise: Tapas 5–14 $.
X-Faktor: Probieren Sie die Spezialität des Hauses: absolut unwiderstehliche Seeigel-Panini.

Intérieur : La belle petite salle avec de hauts plafonds, des miroirs vieillis et un bar sensuel en marbre blanc, a été décorée par Berman Horn Studio.
Horaires d'ouverture : Lun–Jeu 17h–24h (Ven, Sam jusqu'à 1h, Dim jusqu'à 23h). Pas de réservations.
Prix : Tapas 5–14 $.
Le « petit plus » : Ne manquez pas la spécialité de la maison, un délicieux panini aux oursins.

The Odeon

145 West Broadway, New York, NY 10013
☎ +1 212 233 0507
www.theodeonrestaurant.com
Subway: Chambers Street (1, 2, 3, A, C)

There was a time when The Odeon was a lonely outpost of stylish warmth and cheer at the edge of Tribeca. Fast forward nearly three decades, and now restaurateur Keith McNally's original brasserie is one of the few restaurants in New York that deserves to be called a classic. Here, there's always a buzz in the air, and a boldface name or two in the room. Drop in after work for a perfect Martini at the low-lit, Art Deco bar, or for delicious steak frites or roast chicken after midnight.

Einst war das Odeon ein einsamer Außenposten stilvoller Gemütlichkeit am Rand von Tribeca. Drei Jahrzehnte später kann man die Brasserie des Gastronomen Keith McNally mit Recht zu den wenigen Klassikern der New Yorker Restaurantszene zählen. Hier herrscht immer Trubel, und man kann jederzeit ein oder zwei prominente Gesichter entdecken. Die Art-déco-Bar ist der ideale Ort für einen perfekten Martini nach der Arbeit oder für ein delikates Steak Frites oder Roast Chicken nach Mitternacht.

Il fut un temps où l'Odeon était un chaleureux avant-poste d'élégance et de bonne humeur perdu en lisière de Tribeca. Près de 30 ans plus tard, la brasserie de Keith McNally est l'un des rares restaurants de New York à pouvoir se targuer d'être un classique. L'ambiance y est animée et il y a toujours une célébrité ou deux dans la salle. Après le travail, venez prendre un Martini irréprochable à la lumière tamisée du bar Art Déco, ou passez après minuit savourer un délicieux steak frites ou un poulet grillé.

Interior: Art Deco brasserie: high ceilings, mirrors, brown and burgundy leather banquettes, white tablecloths.
Open: Lunch Mon-Fri 11:30am–3pm; brunch Sat-Sun 10am–4pm; dinner Sun-Mon 5:30pm–11pm (Tue-Sat 5:30pm-midnight); brasserie Mon-Fri 3pm–5:30pm, (Sat-Sun 4pm–5:30pm, Thu-Sat noon-1am)
Prices: Lunch $ 15–24; dinner $ 21–34.
X-Factor: After 30 years, still the top choice for late night downtown dining and cocktail schmoozing.

Interieur: Art-déco-Brasserie: hohe Decken, Spiegel, braune und burgunderrote Leder-Sitzbänke, weiße Tischdecken.
Öffnungszeiten: Mo–Mi 11.30–15 Uhr; Brunch Sa/So 10–16 Uhr; Abendessen So/Mo 17.30–23 Uhr, Di–Sa 17.30–24 Uhr; Brasserie Mo–Fr 15–17.30 Uhr, Do–Sa 12–1 Uhr, Sa/So 16–17.30 Uhr.
Preise: Lunch 15–24 $; Dinner 21–34 $.
X-Faktor: Nach 30 Jahren immer noch erste Wahl, wenn nachts warmes Essen oder romantisches Geplauder bei Cocktails gefragt sind.

Intérieur : Brasserie Art Déco : plafonds hauts, miroirs, banquettes en cuir bordeaux et marron, nappes blanches.
Horaires d'ouverture : Déjeuner Lun–Ven 11h30–15h ; brunch Sam–Dim 10h–16h ; dîner Dim–Lun 17h30–23h (Mar–Sam 17h30–24h) ; brasserie Lun–Ven 15h–17h30, (Sam–Dim 16h–17h30, Jeu–Sam 24h–1h)
Prix : Déjeuner 15–24 $; dîner 21–34 $.
Le « petit plus » : Après plusieurs décennies d'existence, c'est encore le meilleur endroit pour dîner tard ou papoter devant un cocktail.

La Esquina

114 Kenmare Street, New York, NY 10012
☎ +1 646 613 7100
www.esquinanyc.com
Subway: Spring Street (6)

Want to start your evening with a bit of an edge? Jump in a cab and head downtown to La Esquina. It looks like a tired old Latin diner from the outside – the signs in the window advertise tacos and empanadas. But then, you're led to a door, down a flight of stairs, through a kitchen, and into a low-lit dining room with a wall full of tequila, and handed a serious menu of Mexican specialties. Once upon a time, La Esquina was indeed the neighborhood dive, but in 2005 architect Derek Sanders and restaurateur James Gersten bought and transformed it into a cool hangout. The coolest thing is that he kept the facade and upstairs part of the original diner intact.

Wollen Sie etwas Salsa in Ihren Abend bringen? Dann lassen Sie sich zum La Esquina fahren. Von außen sieht das Restaurant zwar aus wie ein etwas abgehalftertes Diner – die Reklame wirbt für Tacos und Empanadas –, aber drinnen geht eine Treppe hinunter, mitten durch die Küche in einen schummrigen Speiseraum mit einer Wand voller Tequila. Und hier drückt Ihnen jemand eine Karte mit mexikanischen Spezialitäten in die Hand, die den Namen wirklich verdient. Früher war das La Esquina eine klassische Imbissbude, doch 2005 erwarben Architekt Derek Sanders und Gastronom James Gersten das Restaurant und baute es zu einem coolen Szenetreff um. Becker hat die Fassade und den oberen Bereich des ursprünglichen Diner original erhalten.

D'humeur aventureuse ? Sautez dans un taxi et filez à La Esquina. Avec sa devanture ventant ses tacos et empanadas, on croirait un vieux bouiboui latino. Mais, une fois à l'intérieur, vous descendez un escalier, traversez la cuisine et pénétrez dans une salle à la lumière tamisée où l'on vous tend une carte de plats sophistiqués mexicains. La Esquina était vraiment une gargote de quartier jusqu'en 2005, quand l'architecte Derek Sanders et le restaurateur James Gersten ont fait un lieu branché. L'idée de génie fut de conserver intactes la façade et la salle du rez-de-chaussée.

Interior: An old Latin bodega and diner occupied this downtown corner for decades until co-owners Derek Sanders and James Gersten recreated it as a fine restaurant. **Open: Taqueria** Daily Midday–2am; **Café** Mon–Thu midday–midnight (Fri Midday–1am Sat 11am-1am Sun 11am–11pm); **Brasserie** daily 6pm–2am. **Prices:** Lunch $ 10–20; dinner $ 10–30. **X-Factor:** The kitchen stays open until dawn.

Interieur: Das alte Latino-Diner wurde in ein hervorragendes Restaurant verwandelt. **Öffnungszeiten: Taqueria** tgl. 12–2 Uhr; **Café** Mo–Do 12–24 Uhr, (Fr 12–1 Uhr, Sa 11–1 Uhr, So 11–23 Uhr) ; **Brasserie** täglich 18–2 Uhr. **Preise:** Lunch 10–20 $; Dinner 10–30 $. **X-Faktor:** Die Küche ist durchgehend bis zum Morgengrauen geöffnet.

Intérieur : Les copropriétaires Derek Sanders et James Gersten ont fait un excellent restaurant tout en conservant le décor d'origine. **Horaires d'ouverture : Taqueria** Tous les jours 12h–2h ; **Café** Lun-Jeu 12h-24h, (Ven 12h-1h, Sam 11h-1h, Dim 11h-23h) ; **Brasserie** Lun–Dim 18h–2h. **Prix :** Déjeuner 10–20 $; dîner 10–30 $. **Le « petit plus » :** La cuisine reste ouverte jusqu'à l'aube.

Café Gitane

242 Mott Street, New York, NY 10012
☎ +1 212 334 9552
www.cafegitanenyc.com
Subway: Spring Street (6), Broadway-Lafayette Street (B, D, F, V),
Prince Street (N, R, W)

As you might guess from the familiar looking logo stenciled on the window, this cheap and cheerful Nolita café, opened in 1994, takes its name from the French cigarette brand. The atmosphere is relaxed, comfortable and very Parisian boho. It's classically French in most other ways too – the Mediterranean menu of Moroccan favorites, salades and croques monsieur is almost the same as what you'd find in your favorite place in the Marais. In the afternoons, this place pulls in an arty crowd who come to sip wine, beer, Moroccan mint tea or the good, strong espresso that comes with a square of Belgian chocolate. In the summertime, the action spills out onto the street, around bright-blue café tables.

Dieses preisgünstige Café in Nolita, das 1994 eröffnet wurde, verdankt seinen Namen tatsächlich der französischen Zigarettenmarke (man beachte das Logo) und verströmt eine entspannte, gemütliche und sehr pariserisch anmutende Atmosphäre. Aber auch sonst wirkt es typisch französisch: Die Mittelmeerküche mit marokkanischen Gerichten, die Salades und Croques Monsieur sind nahezu identisch mit den Speisen, die man in seinem Lieblingslokal in Paris serviert bekäme. Nachmittags trifft sich ein künstlerisch angehauchtes Publikum bei Wein, Bier, marokkanischem Minztee oder einem Espresso, der mit einem Stück belgischer Schokolade gereicht wird. Im Sommer verlagert sich das Geschehen auf die Straße an ein paar leuchtend blaue Cafétische mit Sonnenschirmen.

Ce café sympathique et bon marché à Nolita doit son nom aux cigarettes françaises (comme le démontre le logo sur la devanture). Ouvert en 1994, il y règne une ambiance décontractée, confortable, très bohème parisienne. La carte méditerranéenne propose des couscous, des salades et des croque-monsieur si bien qu'on se croirait presque dans un café du Marais. L'après-midi, une clientèle bobo vient y papoter devant un verre de vin, une bière, un thé à la menthe ou un exprès bien tassé accompagné d'un carré de chocolat belge. L'été, on se répand sur le trottoir sous de jolis parasols bleu vif.

Interior: Casual French café-bar, chipped tile floors, scalloped mirrors, formica tables, and there's a bar with barstools.
Open: Sun-Thu 8:30am–midnight, Fri-Sat 8:30am–12:30am.
Prices: Breakfast $ 3–10; lunch and dinner $ 10–14.
X-Factor: If you're on the west side of town, stop by Café Gitane's second location at the Jane Hotel (113 Jane Street).

Interieur: Entspanntes französisches Café, mit brüchigen Fliesenböden, Spiegeln, Resopal-Tischen und einer Bar.
Öffnungszeiten: So–Do 8.30–24 Uhr, Fr/Sa 8.30–0.30 Uhr.
Preise: Frühstück 3–10 $; Lunch und Dinner 10–14 $.
X-Faktor: Wenn Sie auf der West Side unterwegs sind, schauen Sie am zweiten Standort des Café Gitane im Jane Hotel (113 Jane Street) vorbei.

Intérieur : Café bar à la parisienne. Sol en carrelage ébréché, miroirs festonnés, tables en formica et comptoir bordé de tabourets.
Horaires d'ouverture : Dim–Jeu 8h30–24h, Ven/Sam 8h30–0h30
Prix : Petit-déjeuner 3–10 $; déjeuner et dîner 10–14 $.
Le « petit plus » : Si vous passez dans la partie ouest de la ville, arrêtez-vous à la deuxième filiale du Café Gitane, le Jane Hotel (113 Jane Street).

CAFE GITANE

Les apéritifs

Cynar $6.50

Campari $7.50

Noilly Prat $5.00

DELIVERY
5.30 – 11.30

Martini Bianco $5.50

PRIERE DE NE PAS FUMER

Freemans

191 Chrystie Street, New York, NY 10002
☎ +1 212 420 0012
www.freemansrestaurant.com
Subway: Lower East Side-2nd Avenue (F), Bowery (J, M)

Freemans is hidden away at the end of a little alley on the Lower East Side, and it has the allure of a secret speakeasy that you've discovered by accident or word-of-mouth. Inside, the owners have re-created the masculine, clubby atmosphere of a tavern from the era before the American Revolution; antlers and stuffed boar heads decorate the walls; faded Audubon prints of wild birds adorn the space behind the bar. The rustic, hearty comfort food – stews and grilled filet, and three-cheese macaroni – perfectly fits the surroundings, as does the "classic" old-school cocktail menu.

Freemans versteckt sich am Ende einer kleinen Gasse in der Lower East Side und verströmt den Charme einer Flüsterkneipe, die man per Zufall oder durch Mundpropaganda entdeckt hat. Die Besitzer haben hier ein Lokal im maskulinen Klubstil der Zeit vor der Amerikanischen Revolution wieder auferstehen lassen – mitsamt Geweihen und ausgestopften Wildschweinköpfen an den Wänden und verblassten Wildvögel-Drucken hinter der Bar. Das rustikale, herzhafte Essen (Eintöpfe, gegrilltes Filet oder Makkaroni mit drei Käsesorten) passt perfekt in dieses Ambiente, genau wie die Cocktailkarte mit alten „Klassikern".

Caché au fond d'une ruelle du Lower East Side, Freemans rappelle un speakeasy clandestin découvert par hasard ou le bouche à oreille. Ses propriétaires y ont recréé l'atmosphère masculine et intime d'une taverne d'avant la Guerre d'indépendance. Les murs sont ornés de massacres et de têtes de sanglier ; des oiseaux sauvages d'Audubon tapissent l'espace derrière le bar. La cuisine rustique et familiale (ragoûts, filets grillés, macaronis aux trois fromages) est en parfaite harmonie avec le décor, tout comme la carte de bons vieux cocktails d'antan.

Interior: Former halfway house transformed into a "late 1700s tavern" by Taavo Somer and William Tigertt.
Open: Mon–Fri 11am–11:30pm (Sat, Sun brunch from 10am).
Prices: Lunch $ 6–16; dinner $ 13–26.
X-Factor: Be sure to try the unique signature dish, "Devils on Horseback" – bacon-wrapped prunes stuffed with Stilton cheese.

Interieur: Ehemaliges Übergangsheim für Strafgefangene, von Taavo Somer und William Tigertt liebevoll in ein „Gasthaus des späten 17. Jahrhunderts" verwandelt.
Öffnungszeiten: Mo–Fr 11–23.30 Uhr. (Sa, So Brunch ab 10 Uhr).
Preise: Lunch 6–16 $; Dinner 13–26 $.
X-Faktor: Man sollte auf jeden Fall die „Devils on Horseback" probieren: mit Stilton gefüllte Backpflaumen im Speckmantel.

Intérieur : Ancien foyer de transition reconverti en « taverne de la fin du 17e siècle » par les propriétaires et designers Taavo Somer et William Tigertt.
Horaires d'ouverture : Lun–Ven 11h–23h30. (Sam, Dim brunch à partir de 10h).
Prix : Déjeuner 6–16 $; dîner 13–26 $.
Le « petit plus » : Ne repartez pas sans essayer « Devils on Horseback », des pruneaux farcis au Stilton et enrobés de bacon.

Schiller's Liquor Bar

131 Rivington Street, New York, NY 10002
☎ +1 212 260 4555
www.schillersny.com
Subway: Delancey Street (F), Essex Street (J, M, Z)

This relaxed Lower East Side bistro, opened in 2003, has all the signature touches of master New York restaurateur Keith McNally (owner of Pastis, Balthazar, and founder of Odeon). The setting is as painstakingly art directed as a movie set – this one's an updated version of a turn-of-the-century saloon. The bistro-style French, English and American food is unpretentious – the wine list is divided into "cheap, decent and good" categories. The atmosphere changes depending on when you drop in – on Saturday nights, it's one of the best parties in town, on a late afternoon, aromantic rendezvous.

Dieses 2003 eröffnete, entspannte Bistro in der Lower East Side trägt die Handschrift des Meistergastronomen Keith McNally (Eigner des Pastis und Balthazar und Gründer des Odeon). Der Raum ist gestylt wie ein Filmset – die moderne Version eines Saloons der Jahrhundertwende. Die Bistrokarte mit französischen, englischen und amerikanischen Snacks ist bodenständig, und die Weinkarte unterteilt sich in „billig", „ordentlich" und „gut". Die Atmosphäre wechselt mit der Tageszeit – samstagabends tobt hier eine der besten Partys der Stadt, spätnachmittags kann man hier ein romantisches Rendezvous genießen.

Ce bistrot du Lower East Side ouvert en 2003 porte la griffe du restaurateur Keith McNally (propriétaire de Pastis, Balthazar et fondateur de l'Odeon). Le décor y est aussi soigné que sur un plateau de cinéma : une reconstitution modernisée d'un resto ouvrier du début du siècle. La cuisine de type brasserie est sans prétention. La carte des vins est divisée en « pas cher, pas mal et bon ». L'ambiance dépend du moment : le samedi soir, la fête bat son plein ; en fin d'après-midi, c'est l'idéal pour un rendez-vous amoureux.

Interior: Designed by Keith McNally with his regular design partners, Ian McPheely and Christian Garnett.
Open: Mon–Wed 11am–1am (Thu till 2am, Fri, Sat till 3am); Sat 10am–3am (Sun till 1am).
Prices: Breakfast and lunch $ 7–19; dinner $ 8–29.
X-Factor: Schiller's not only mixes some of the stiffest drinks in town; they also offer WiFi internet.

Interieur: Die Bar wurde von Keith McNally und seinen Partnern Ian McPheely und Christian Garnett entworfen.
Öffnungszeiten: Mo–Mi 11–1 Uhr (Do bis 2, Fr, Sa bis 3 Uhr); Sa 10–3 Uhr (So bis 1 Uhr).
Preise: Frühstück und Lunch 7–19 $; Dinner 8–29 $.
X-Faktor: Das Schiller's mixt nicht nur einige der hochtourigsten Drinks der Stadt, sondern bietet auch Internetzugang per WiFi.

Intérieur : Décoré par Keith McNally avec ses partenaires habituels, Ian McPheely et Christian Garnett.
Horaires d'ouverture : Lun–Mer 11h–1h (Jeu, jusqu'à 2h, Ven, Sam jusqu'à 3h) ; Sam 10h–3h (Dim jusqu'à 1h).
Prix : Petit-déjeuner et déjeuner 7–19 $; dîner 8–29 $.
Le « petit plus » : On y trouve les cocktails les plus corsés de la ville.

Charlie Bird

5 King Street (entrance on 6th Avenue), New York City, NY 10012
☎ +1 212 235 7133
www.charliebirdnyc.com
Subway: Spring Street (C, E)

The restaurant's name is a reminder of jazz saxophonist Charles "Bird" Parker, famed for his expressive style. The walls of the dining area feature photographs by Lyle Owerko, who has captured hip hoppers' and breakdancers' boomboxes almost as if they were fossils from the Cretaceous period. Street culture in New York is now a growing retro trend. The cuisine is Italian, and all the ingredients are bred or farmed organically. The wine list in Charlie Bird is particularly interesting, as one of the owners, Robert Bohr, was formerly the sommelier in the now closed restaurant Cru. His recommendations are certainly reliable. New Yorkers swear by the Farro Salad, incidentally, which has even featured as a recipe in the New York Times. It is made with cooked farro grains, tomatoes, refreshing sliced radish, and fruity olive oil.

Interior: Wedge heel shaped dining area. The yellow faux leather banquettes are attractive, without being too conspicuous.
Open: Mon-Thu 5.30pm–11pm, Fri midday –3pm & 5.30pm–midnight, Sat 11am–3pm & 5.30pm–midnight, Sun 11am–3pm & 5.30pm–11pm.
Prices: Lunch $ 16–22, dinner $10–39, spring lamb ragu rigatoni $ 20.
X-Factor: The restaurant is very popular, but the dining area is small. Come early!

Der Name des Restaurants erinnert an den Saxofonisten Charles Parker, berühmt für seinen expressiven Stil. Im Gastraum hängen Fotografien von Lyle Owerko, der die Kassettenrekorder der Hip-Hopper und Breakdancer so monumental ablichtet, als handelte es sich um Fossilien aus der Kreidezeit. In New York besinnt man sich zunehmend auf die sogenannte Street Culture. Die Küche ist italienisch, und die Zutaten stammen aus biodynamischer Landwirtschaft. Besonders interessant ist die Weinkarte (einer der Inhaber, Robert Bohr, war zuvor Sommelier im Restaurant Cru). Vertrauen Sie sich seinen Empfehlungen an! Die New Yorker schwören übrigens auf den Faro Salad, dessen Rezept es schon in die New York Times gebracht hat: Dinkelweizen mit Tomaten, Radieschenscheiben und fruchtigem Olivenöl.

Interieur: Der Gastraum hat die Form eines Wedge Heels. Die durchgehende Sitzbank mit gelbem Kunstlederpolster fällt da zwar kaum, dennoch angenehm auf.
Öffnungszeiten: Mo–Do 17:30–23 Uhr; Fr 12–15 Uhr & 17:30–0 Uhr, Sa 11–15 & 17:30–0 Uhr, So 11–15 Uhr 17:30–23 Uhr.
Preise: Lunch 16–22 $, Dinner 10–39 $, Rigatoni mit Lammragout 20 $
X-Faktor: Das Restaurant ist sehr beliebt, der Gastraum aber klein. Kommen Sie zeitig!

Le nom du restaurant rend hommage au saxophoniste Charles Parker, célèbre pour son style très expressif. Les murs sont ornés de photographies par Lyle Owerko, qui donne aux magnétophones des danseurs de hip-hop et de break dance le caractère monumental de fossiles du crétacé. À New York, on aime de plus en plus se souvenir de la Street Culture. La cuisine est italienne et tous les ingrédients sont issus de l'agriculture biodynamique. Mais c'est la carte des vins qui est particulièrement intéressante au Charlie Bird, car l'un des propriétaires, Robert Bohr, a été sommelier au restaurant Cru. Fiez-vous à ses conseils ! Les New-Yorkais ne jurent sinon que par la Faro Salad, dont il a aussi publié la recette dans le New York Times. Il s'agit d'épeautre cuit aux tomates, radis rafraîchissantes et huile d'olive fruitée.

Intérieur : La salle a la forme d'un talon compensé. Le banc en simili-cuir jaune se fait peu remarquer, mais est agréable à l'œil.
Horaires d'ouverture : Lun–Jeu 17 h 30–23 h ; Ven 12 h–15 h & 17 h 30–0 h ; Sam 11 h–15 h & 17 h 30–0 h ; Dim 11 h–15 h & 17 h 30–23 h.
Prix : Lunch 16–22 $, dîner 10–39 $, rigatoni et ragoût d'agneau 20 $.
Le « petit plus » : Le restaurant est très apprécié. Venez tôt pour éviter d'attendre.

Katz's Delicatessen

---

205 East Houston Street, New York, NY 10002
☎ +1 212 254 2246
www.katzdeli.com

Subway: Lower East Side-2nd Avenue (F, V)

Katz's deli was established in 1888, when the Lower East Side was the first landing point for hundreds of thousands of East European Jewish immigrants. To say it's an institution is an understatement – for many people, this "joint" with its workingman's bare tables, walls covered with snapshots of the owners with their arms around everybody from Bill Clinton to Jerry Lewis, represents the essence of classic New York. But the biggest stars here are the sandwiches made with special rye bread, stuffed to bursting with 400 grams of pastrami, corned beef (or both!) that's been specially dry-cured for 30 days.

Katz's Delicatessen eröffnete 1888, als die Lower East Side der erste Anlaufpunkt für Hunderttausende jüdischer Immigranten aus Osteuropa war. Katz's als Institution zu bezeichnen, ist fast schon untertrieben. Für viele Menschen bildet dieser Treffpunkt mit den blanken Tischen und unzähligen Bildern der Besitzer und berühmter Gäste, wie Bill Clinton und Jerry Lewis, schlicht den Inbegriff des alten New York. Die größten Stars sind hier allerdings die Sandwiches aus einem besonderen Roggenbrot, prall gefüllt mit 400 Gramm Pastrami oder Corned Beef (oder beidem), die 30 Tage lang in einem speziellen Verfahren gepökelt wurden.

Katz's Delicatessen a été fondé en 1888, quand le Lower East Side était une terre d'accueil pour des centaines de milliers d'immigrants juifs d'Europe de l'Est. C'est plus qu'une institution : avec ses tables nues, ses murs tapissés de photos des propriétaires bras dessus bras dessous avec des célébrités, de Bill Clinton à Jerry Lewis, c'est la quintessence du vieux New York. Mais les vraies stars ici, ce sont les sandwichs au pain de seigle bourrés à craquer de 400 grammes de pastrami, de corned-beef (ou des deux !) salé à sec pendant 30 jours.

Interior: Classic deli grunge: hanging salamis, formica tables, overhead fluorescent tube lighting.
Open: Mon –Tue 8am–9:45pm (Wed–Thu, Sun till 10:45pm, Fri–Sat till 2:45 am).
Prices: Breakfast $ 4–15; lunch, dinner $ 6–30.
X-Factor: This is where Meg Ryan had her famous fake orgasm in the film When Harry Met Sally.

Interieur: Klassische Deli-Einrichtung mit aufgehängten Salamis, Resopal-Tischen und Neonbeleuchtung.
Öffnungszeiten: Mo–Di 8–21.45 Uhr (Mi–Do, So bis 22.45 Uhr, Fr–Sa bis 2.45 Uhr).
Preise: Frühstück 4–15 $; Lunch, Dinner 6–30 $.
X-Faktor: Hier hatte Meg Ryan in Harry und Sally ihren berühmten vorgetäuschten Orgasmus.

Intérieur : Classique bistrot ouvrier : salamis suspendus, tables en formica, tubes de néon au plafond.
Horaires d'ouverture : Lun–Mar 8h–21h45 (Mer–Jeu, Dim jusqu'à 22h45, Ven–Sam jusqu'à 2h45).
Prix : Petit-déjeuner 4–15 $; déjeuner et dîner 6–30 $.
Le « petit plus » : C'est ici que Meg Ryan a feint l'orgasme dans la fameuse scène de Quand Harry rencontre Sally.

Pure Food & Wine

54 Irving Place, New York, NY 10003
☎ +1 212 477 1010
www.purefoodandwine.com
Subway: 14th Street-Union Square (L, N, Q, R, W, 4, 5, 6)

They are not kidding about the "Pure". Everything served at this Gramercy Park restaurant, opened in 2004, is organic, raw and vegan. The surprise is that this super-healthy food is also delicious, beautifully prepared, and sophisticated haute cuisine – it is even a favorite of Diane von Furstenberg's. The owner, Sarma Melngailis, is a grad of the French Culinary Institute and the author of two raw food cookbooks; the menu includes tempting and totally original concoctions like a mushroom and hempseed burger, and zucchini and heirloom tomato lasagna with basil pistachio pesto.

Das Pure macht seinem Namen alle Ehre: Alles in diesem 2004 eröffneten Gramercy-Park-Restaurant ist biologisch angebaut, roh und vegan. Überraschenderweise schmeckt dieses megagesunde Essen nicht nur hervorragend, sondern ist auch noch schön zubereitet und definitiv Haute Cuisine – Diane von Furstenberg gehört zu den Stammgästen. Eignerin Sarma Melngailis hat am französischen Institut Culinaire gelernt und zwei Rohkostkochbücher geschrieben. Die Karte bietet köstliche und originelle Kreationen, wie Pilz- und Hanfsamen-Burger sowie Lasagne von Zucchini und alten Tomatensorten mit Basilikum-Pistazien-Pesto.

Ils ne plaisantent pas avec la « pureté ». Tout ce qui est servi dans ce restaurant de Gramercy Park ouvert en 2004 est bio, cru et végétalien. Non seulement c'est sain mais c'est de la haute cuisine délicieuse et superbement présentée. Diane von Furstenberg en raffole. La propriétaire, Sarma Melngailis, est diplômée du French Culinary Institute et l'auteur de deux livres de recettes crues. La carte inclut des créations surprenantes et tentantes comme le burger aux champignons et graines de chanvre ou les lasagnes aux courgettes et aux tomates avec un pesto au basilic et à la pistache.

Interior: Understated, modern, wood paneled walls; outdoor seating in a private garden, designed by the owner.
Open: Lunch Mon-Sun 12pm-4pm; dinner 5:30pm-11pm; brunch Sat-Sun 12pm-4pm
Prices: Dinner $ 23–26.
X-Factor: The fresh-pressed juice cocktails, made with organic sake.

Interieur: Zurückgenommen, modern mit holzgetäfelten Wänden. Terrasse im Privatgarten, von der Eignerin selbst entworfen.
Öffnungszeiten: Mittagessen tgl. 12–16 Uhr, Abendessen 17.30–23 Uhr, Brunch Sa/So 12–16 Uhr
Preise: Dinner 23–26 $.
X-Faktor: Die frisch gepressten Fruchtcocktails mit Bio-Sake.

Intérieur : Conçu par la propriétaire. Discret et moderne, avec des murs lambrissés et des tables dans un jardin privé.
Horaires d'ouverture : Déjeuner Lun–Dim 12h–16h ; dîner 17h30–23h ; brunch Sam–Dim 12h–16h.
Le « petit plus » : Les cocktails de fruits fraîchement pressés au saké bio.

City Bakery

3 West 18th Street, New York, NY 10011
☎ +1 212 366 1414
www.thecitybakery.com

Subway: 18th Street (1), 14th Street (F, V),
14 Street-Union Square (L, N, Q, R, W, 4, 5, 6)

The City Bakery, opened in 1990, is a block away from the Greenmarket, New York's renowned open-air farmer's market. It's a great stop if you're in need of a quick and very healthy meal. The City Bakery's lunch, snack, tea and light supper menu offers seasonal snacks, sandwiches and salads, based on locally-sourced and organic food (much of it from the nearby Greenmarket). It's also a wonderful place to indulge your sweet tooth with one of the City Bakery's house specialties: hot chocolate, brownies, chocolate croissants, and the unusual pretzel croissant.

Die 1990 eröffnete City Bakery liegt nur einen Block von New Yorks berühmten Wochenmarkt, dem Greenmarket, entfernt. Wem der Sinn nach etwas Kleinem und Gesundem steht, ist hier genau richtig. Da alles Self-service ist, geht es auch noch schnell. Auf der Karte der City Bakery stehen je nach Saison wechselnde Snacks, Sandwiches und Salate aus lokalem und ökologischem Anbau (vieles stammt vom nahen Greenmarket), aber auch alles, was das Herz eines jeden Schokoholics höher schlagen lässt: heiße Schokolade (man sagt die beste in der Stadt), Brownies, Schoko-Croissants und das ungewöhnliche Bretzel-Croissant.

Ouvert en 1990, la City Bakery n'est qu'à deux pas de Greenmarket, le fameux marché de producteurs de Manhattan. C'est l'endroit idéal si vous voulez un repas rapide et très sain. La carte propose des en-cas, des sandwichs et des salades composés d'ingrédients locaux frais et bio (la plupart proviennent de Greenmarket). Et si vous avez le bec sucré, ne manquez pas de goûter à une des spécialités de la maison : le chocolat chaud, le brownie, le croissant au chocolat ou, une originalité, le croissant bretzel.

Interior: Principal design by baker Maury Rubin and savory chef Ilene Rosen.
Open: Mon–Sat 7:30am–7pm; Sun 9am–6pm.
Prices: Breakfast: $ 3–5; lunch $ 10–15; hot chocolate: $ 2–5.
X-Factor: The pretzel croissant, a sweet and salty pastry with a cult following and its own website: www.pretzelcroissant.com.

Interieur: Für das Design sind vor allem die Konditorin Maury Rubin und die Küchenchefin Ilene Rosen verantwortlich.
Öffnungszeiten: Mo–Sa 7.30–19 Uhr; So 9–18 Uhr.
Preise: Frühstück: 3–5 $; Lunch 10–15 $; Hot Chocolate 2–5 $.
X-Faktor: Das Bretzel Croissant, ein salziges und süßes Gebäck, das bereits Kultstatus und eine eigene Website hat: www.pretzelcroissant.com.

Intérieur : Design principal dû au boulanger-pâtissier Maury Rubin et à la chef Ilene Rosen.
Horaires d'ouverture : Lun–Sam 7h30–19h ; Dim 9h–18h.
Prix : Petit déjeuner 3–5 $; déjeuner 10–15 $; chocolat chaud 2–5 $.
Le « petit plus » : Le croissant bretzel, une pâtisserie salée-sucrée unique qui a son propre site Web : www.pretzelcroissant.com.

Shake Shack

Madison Square Park
Madison Avenue at 23rd Street, New York, NY 10010
☎ +1 212 889 6600
www.shakeshack.com
Subway: 23rd Street (R, W, 6)

The Shake Shack is a beautiful, no-pretensions place to sit in the summer and enjoy a burger and fries under the leafy trees of Madison Square Park. And its not just any burger: the Shake Shack was created by Danny Meyer and is part of the Union Square restaurant group that includes the haute Gramercy Tavern. So the ingredients are tops, and so is the taste – try one of the all-beef hot dogs, served on a poppy-seed bun. Wash it down with homemade lemonade, or a gourmet root beer from Louisiana. For less than 10 dollars, you can't do better than this.

Das Shake Shack ist ein herrlich unprätentiöser Ort, um im Sommer unter den Bäumen des Madison Square Park einen Burger mit Fritten zu genießen – aber nicht irgendeinen Burger: Der von Danny Meyer geschaffene Imbiss ist Teil der Union-Square-Restaurantgruppe, zu der auch die gehobene Gramercy Tavern gehört. Zutaten und Geschmack sind also erstklassig – man probiere nur einmal ein Rindfleisch-Hotdog im Mohnbrötchen. Dazu passt hausgemachte Limonade oder ein Gourmet Root Beer aus Louisiana. Besser geht es für unter 10 Dollar einfach nicht.

Le Shake Shack est un charmant kiosque sans prétention où déguster un hamburger à l'ombre des grands arbres du Madison Square Park. Et pas n'importe quel hamburger : créé par Danny Meyer, le Shack appartient au groupe Union Square Hospitality qui inclut la Gramercy Tavern, étoilée au Michelin. Les ingrédients sont donc de premier ordre. Goûtez un des hot-dogs pur bœuf dans un petit pain aux graines de pavot, arrosé d'une limonade faite maison ou d'une root beer de Louisiane. Pour moins de 10 dollars, il n'y a pas mieux.

Interior: Sleek modern kiosk designed by SITE Environmental Design; alfresco tables under the trees.
Open: Mon–Sun 11am–11pm.
Prices: $ 5–9. A double Shack Burger is approx. $ 8.
X-Factor: A portion of the profits are donated to the Madison Square Park Conservancy.

Interieur: Schicker moderner Imbiss mit Tischen unter den Bäumen, entworfen von SITE Environmental Design.
Öffnungszeiten: Mo–So 11.30 Uhr – 21.30 Uhr.
Preise: 5–9 $. Der Double Shack Burger kostet ca. 8 $.
X-Faktor: Ein Teil der Einnahmen geht an die Initiative Madison Square Park Conservancy zur Verschönerung des Parks.

Intérieur : Kiosque moderne épuré conçu par SITE Environmental Design ; tables sous les arbres.
Horaires d'ouverture : Lun–Dim 11h–23h.
Prix : 5–9 $. Un double Shack Burger env. 8 $.
Le « petit plus » : Une part des bénéfices est reversée au Madison Square Park Conservancy.

Market Café

496 9th Avenue, New York, NY 10018
☎ +1 212 967 3892
www.marketcafenyc.com
Subway: 34th Street-Penn Station (A, C, E)

The Market Café's clean, casual retro look – turquoise banquettes and formica tables, a long counter with vintage soda-fountain bar stools – makes you think, immediately: burgers and fries. But appearances can be deceiving. This restaurant, which opened on the edge of the Hell's Kitchen neighborhood in 1993, is no mere diner, it has a serious American-continental menu, with reasonable prices and a relaxed atmosphere. And there's another plus: the Market Café is one of the few reliable choices for dinner in this area near the sports and concert arena Madison Square Garden, and the repertory theaters of West 42nd Street.

Das schlichte, unangestrengte Retro-Design des Market Café – türkisfarbene Bänke und Resopal-Tische, ein langer Tresen mit altmodischen Barhockern – lässt einen unwillkürlich an Hamburger und Fritten denken. Aber der Eindruck täuscht: Dieses 1993 am Rand von Hell's Kitchen eröffnete Restaurant ist kein simples Diner, sondern ein Lokal mit ernst zu nehmender amerikanischer Küche zu vernünftigen Preisen in entspannter Atmosphäre. Dazu kommt, dass das Market Café zu den wenigen zuverlässigen Dinner-Restaurants in der Nähe des Madison Square Garden und der Theater an der West 42nd Street zählt.

Le look rétro et décontracté du Market Café (banquettes turquoises, tables en formica, long comptoir bordé de hauts tabourets) fait immédiatement penser : « hamburger frites ». Ne vous y trompez pas : ce restaurant ouvert en 1993 en lisière de Hell's Kitchen sert une cuisine américaine sérieuse à des prix abordables dans une ambiance détendue. L'autre plus : c'est l'une des rares tables fiables dans ce quartier près du Madison Square Garden et des théâtres de West 42nd Street.

Interior: Updated 1950s New York diner, with original white tile walls, located in a former butcher shop; designed by architect Robert Goodwin.
Open: Mon–Tue midday–10pm (Wed–Sat till 11pm); Sun 11am–4pm.
Prices: Lunch, dinner $ 14–20.
X-Factor: It is one of the few New York restaurants that will cheerfully prepare special meals for people with food sensitivities and allergies.

Interieur: Renoviertes Diner aus den 1950ern mit original erhaltenen weiß gekachelten Wänden in einer ehemaligen Metzgerei, entworfen von Robert Goodwin.
Öffnungszeiten: Mo–Di 12–22 Uhr (Mi–Sa bis 23 Uhr); So 11–16 Uhr.
Preise: Lunch, Dinner 14–20 $.
X-Faktor: Eines der wenigen New Yorker Restaurants, die gern spezielle Speisen für Menschen mit Lebensmittelunverträglich-keiten und Allergien zubereiten.

Intérieur : Diner des années 1950 modernisé, situé dans une ancienne boucherie. Conçu par l'architecte Robert Goodwin.
Horaires d'ouverture : Lun–Mar 12h–22h (Mer–Sam jusqu'à 23h); Dim 11h–16h.
Prix : Déjeuner, dîner 14–20 $.
Le « petit plus » : Un des rares restaurants à New-York qui accepte volontiers d'adapter ses plats pour les personnes souffrant de problèmes d'alimentation et d'allergies.

Esca

402 West 43rd Street, New York, NY 10036
☎ +1 212 564 7272
www.esca-nyc.com

Subway: 42nd Street-Port Authority Bus Terminal (A, C, E)

The owner of this midtown favorite, Dave Pasternack, is a fisherman – and he also was voted "Best New York Chef of the Year" by the James Beard Foundation. As you'd expect, his first effort as restaurateur (with Mario Batali and Joe Bastianich) is all about the seafood. Esca's is considered by many to be the best in the city – it's fresh, and perfectly prepared in the southern Italian style. The restaurant earned three stars from the New York Times dining critic, and you'll often find editors and writers from the newspaper lunching here (their new skyscraper, designed by Renzo Piano, is just a few steps away).

Dave Pasternack, der Besitzer dieses äußerst beliebten Midtown-Restaurants, ist Fischer von Beruf – und wurde außerdem von der James Beard Foundation zum „Best New York Chef of the Year" ernannt. Natürlich dreht sich in seinem ersten Restaurant, das er zusammen mit Mario Batali and Joe Bastianich betreibt, alles um Fisch und Meeresfrüchte. Das Esca gilt bei vielen Kennern als bestes Fischrestaurant der Stadt. So verlieh der Restaurantkritiker der New York Times drei Sterne – was ein Grund dafür sein könnte, dass viele Redakteure und Autoren der Zeitung regelmäßig hier essen (außerdem liegt das neue, von Renzo Piano entworfene Verlags-Hochhaus nur wenige Schritte entfernt).

Dave Pasternack, pêcheur et propriétaire de ce restaurant très prisé de Midtown, a été élu « meilleur chef new-yorkais de l'année » par la fondation James Beard. Associé à Mario Batali et Joe Bastianich, il a donc concentré tous ses efforts sur le poisson et celui d'Esca est souvent considéré comme le meilleur de la ville : toujours frais et préparé à merveille comme en Italie du Sud. Le restaurant a reçu trois étoiles dans la rubrique gastronomique du New York Times et l'on voit souvent ses éditeurs et journalistes y déjeuner. (Leur nouveau gratte-ciel, conçu par Renzo Piano, est à deux pas.)

Interior: Modern, uncomplicated space, beige and brown tones, wood floors, outdoor garden, designed by Lisa Eaton.
Open: Tue–Sat midday–2:30pm and 5pm–11:30pm (Mon till 10:30pm); Sun 4:30pm–10:30pm.
Prices: Lunch $ 23–30; dinner $ 24–37.
X-Factor: Make sure to sample Esca's specialty, the "crudo" – raw fish served Italian style – a rarity on New York menus.

Interieur: Moderne, unkomplizierte Räumlichkeiten in Beige- und Brauntönen, dazu Holzböden und ein Garten.
Öffnungszeiten: Di–Sa 12–14.30 Uhr und 7–23.30 Uhr (Mo bis 22.30 Uhr); So 16.30–22.30 Uhr.
Preise: Lunch 23–30 $; Dinner 24–37 $.
X-Faktor: Probieren Sie unbedingt die Esca-Spezialität „crudo" – roher Fisch auf italienische Art –, die ansonsten kaum auf New Yorker Speisekarten zu finden ist.

Intérieur : Espace moderne et épuré, tons beige et marron, parquets, jardin.
Horaires d'ouverture : Mar–Sam 12h–14h30 et 17h–23h30 (Lun jusqu'à 22h30); Dim 16h30–22h30h.
Prix : Déjeuner 23–30 $; dîner 24–37 $.
Le « petit plus » : Goûtez la spécialité de la maison, le « crudo », du poisson cru préparé à l'italienne. On en trouve très rarement dans les restaurants à New York.

Keens Steakhouse

72 West 36th Street, New York, NY 10018
☎ +1 212 947 3636
www.keens.com
Subway: 34th Street-Herald Square (B, D, F, N, Q, R)

There are times, in New York City, when nothing else will do but a succulent and juicy New York Strip Steak. There are several steak houses that vie for the crown of "best steak in the city", but Keens is always at the top of the list. It has wonderfully aged and perfectly grilled meat, and the ambience is rich with the history of old New York. Founded in 1885 as a pipe club, Keens didn't admit women until 1905 – Lillie Langtry, the actress and paramour of future King Edward VII, sued for access, and won her case. The list of colorful Keens' habitues is long: J. P. Morgan, architect Stanford White, Theodore Roosevelt, "Buffalo Bill" Cody and even Albert Einstein.

Manchmal muss es einfach ein saftiges New York Strip Steak sein! Zwar wetteifern gleich mehrere Steakhäuser in New York um die Auszeichnung „Bestes Steak der Stadt", aber das Keens steht immer ganz oben auf der Liste. Hier gibt es erstklassig abgehangenes und perfekt gegrilltes Fleisch, und das Ambiente atmet New Yorker Geschichte. Das Keens wurde 1885 als Pfeifenraucherklub gegründet und ließ Frauen erst 1905 zu, nachdem Lillie Langtry, Schauspielerin und Mätresse des künftigen Königs Edward VII., sich eingeklagt hatte. Zu den Stammgästen des Keens zählten Persönlichkeiten wie J. P. Morgan, Architekt Stanford White, Theodore Roosevelt, „Buffalo Bill" Cody und sogar Albert Einstein.

Certains jours, à Manhattan, une bonne coquille d'aloyau saignante s'impose. Plusieurs grills rivalisent pour le titre de meilleure « steak house » mais Keens l'emporte haut la main. Le lieu est patiné, la viande parfaitement grillée et l'ambiance riche de l'histoire du vieux New York. Fondé en 1885 comme club de fumeurs de pipe, les femmes n'y ont été admises qu'en 1905. Lillie Langtry, actrice et maîtresse du futur Édouard VII, leur a fait un procès et a gagné. La liste des habitués célèbres est longue, incluant J. P. Morgan, l'architecte Stanford White, Roosevelt, Buffalo Bill et même Einstein.

Interior: Rustic tavern. Walls covered with historical ephemera – including a theater program Abraham Lincoln held when he was assassinated. Design by Austrian artist Kiki Kogelnik.
Open: Mon–Fri 11:45am–10:30pm; Sat 5pm–10:30pm (Sun till 9:30 pm).
Prices: Lunch $ 24–57; dinner $ 24–82 $.
X-Factor: The ceilings display the world's largest claypipe collection.

Interieur: Rustikaler Tavernenstil, an den Wänden historische Souvenirs – wie das Theaterprogramm, das Abraham Lincoln bei seiner Ermordung hielt. Entworfen von der österreichischen Künstlerin Kiki Kogelnik.
Öffnungszeiten: Mo–Fr 11.45–22.30 Uhr; Sa 17–22.30 Uhr (So bis 21 Uhr).
Preise: Lunch 24–57 $; Dinner 24–82 $.
X-Faktor: An der Decke prangt die größte Tonpfeifensammlung der Welt.

Intérieur : Taverne rustique de la fin du 19e siècle. Murs tapissés de documents historiques, dont le programme de théâtre que tenait Abraham quand il fut assassiné.
Horaires d'ouverture : Lun–Ven 11h45–22h30 ; Sam 17h–22h30 (Dim jusqu'à 21h30).
Prix : Déjeuner 24–57 $; dîner 24–82 $.
Le « petit plus » : Les plafonds sont tapissés de la plus grande collection de pipes au monde.

Grand Central Oyster Bar & Restaurant

Grand Central Station, New York, NY 10017
☎ +1 212 490 6650
www.oysterbarny.com
Subway: Grand Central-42nd Street (S, 4, 5, 6, 7)

One of New York's grand old establishments, the Oyster Bar & Restaurant opened its doors in 1913. Located in the lower concourse of the magnificent, cathedral-like Beaux Arts Grand Central railroad terminal, the Oyster Bar is an absolute must stop. Take a seat at the long counter and order from an ever-changing selection of more than 30 different kinds of raw oysters from California, British Columbia, Rhode Island, Prince Edward Island and Virginia. Make sure to leave room for a bowl of the signature Manhattan clam chowder, served with a packet of "oyster" crackers.

Das Oyster Bar & Restaurant ist eine von New Yorks ehrwürdigsten Einrichtungen und öffnete seine Türen bereits 1913. In der unteren Bahnhofshalle des kathedralenartigen Beaux-Arts-Bahnhofs Grand Central Station ist die Oyster Bar ein absolutes Muss für jeden New-York-Besucher. An der langen Bar sitzend, sollte jeder einmal eine der über 30 verschiedenen und stets wechselnden Austernsorten aus Kalifornien, British Columbia, Rhode Island, Prince Edward Island oder Virginia probiert haben. Dazu gehört der berühmte Manhattan Clam Chowder, der mit einem Paket „Oyster-Crackers" serviert wird.

Le vénérable Oyster Bar & Restaurant, un des monuments de Manhattan, a ouvert ses portes en 1913. Situé dans le hall inférieur de Grand Central, la magnifique et monumentale gare de style Beaux-Arts, il vaut vraiment le détour. Installez-vous au long comptoir et choisissez dans la sélection toujours changeante d'une trentaine de types d'huîtres provenant de Californie, de Colombie Britannique, du Rhode Island, de Virginie et de l'île-du-Prince-Édouard. Gardez un peu de place pour le fameux Manhattan clam chowder (bisque de palourdes), servi avec un paquet de crackers salés.

Interior: There's an open counter, and a sit-down restaurant, both under magnificent vaulted white-tiled ceilings.
Open: Mon–Sat 11:30am-9:30pm.
Prices: Oysters are $ 2–3 per piece; dinner entrees are around $ 29.
X-Factor: Ask them to show you the spot under the arch, where you can whisper to a friend standing 20 feet away.

Interieur: Unter dem fantastischen, weiß gefliesten Deckengewölbe finden sich Bartresen sowie ein Restaurant mit Tischen.
Öffnungszeiten: Mo–Sa 11:30.
Preise: Austern 2–3 $ pro Stück; Hauptgerichte um 29 $.
X-Faktor: Man sollte sich die Stelle unter dem Bogen zeigen lassen, von der aus ein Flüstern in sechs Metern Entfernung zu hören ist.

Intérieur : Comptoir et tables sous de magnifiques plafonds voûtés tapissés de carreaux blancs.
Horaires d'ouverture : Lun–Sam 11h30–21h30.
Prix : Les huîtres coûtent 2 à 3 $ l'unité ; plats principaux autour de 29 $.
Le « petit plus » : Demandez-leur de vous montrer l'endroit sous l'arche où vous pouvez chuchoter et vous faire entendre à six mètres.

STEW / PANROAST | BLU
OYSTER $10.45 | BEL
CHERRYSTONE $13.25 | BLA
IPSWICH $14.45 | COT
SCALLOP $13.75 | COT
SHRIMP $14.45 | GREA
LOBSTER $22.75 | GLID
COMBINATION $21.45 | HAM
| ISI
MALEPEQUE | KUM
| MOO

The Four Seasons Restaurant

99 East 52nd Street, New York, NY 10022
☎ +1 212 754 9494
www.FourSeasonsRestaurant.com
Subway: 51st Street (6), Lexington Avenue/53rd Street (E, V)

You don't come to the Four Seasons Restaurant merely to eat – you come to worship at the temple of International Style. Located in Ludwig Mies van der Rohe's landmark Seagram building, Mies teamed with fellow architectural luminary Philip Johnson to design every detail of New York's greatest dining room in accordance with less is more principles. Everything else, from the seating (Mies, Eero Saarinen, Eames) to the champagne glasses (by Garth and Ada Louise Huxtable) was designed by Modernist notables. The contemporary cuisine is as stunning as the decor. Lunch at the Grill Room has been a ritual for New York's glitterati and power-brokers since the restaurant's opening in 1959 – John Kennedy had his 45th birthday party here in 1962.

Ins Four Seasons Restaurant geht man nicht nur, um zu essen, sondern um diesen Tempel des International Style zu bestaunen. Jedes Detail im groß-artigsten Speisezimmer New Yorks wurde nach dem Grundsatz „weniger ist mehr" von Architektur-Ikone Philip Johnson gestaltet, der sich dazu mit Mies van der Rohe zusammentat, der übrigens das gesamte Seagram-Gebäu-de entwarf, in dem sich das Restaurant befindet. Die Ausstattung, von den Stühlen (Mies, Eero Saarinen, Eames) bis zu den Champagnergläsern (Garth und Ada Louise Huxtable), ist minde-stens genauso hochkarätig wie auch die zeitgenössisch Küche des Hauses. Lunch im Grill Room gehört seit der Eröffnung 1959 zu den Ritualen der Schickeria und Börsenmakler-Elite: So feierte John F. Kennedy 1962 hier sei-nen 45. Geburtstag.

On ne vient pas au restaurant du Four Seasons que pour manger mais aussi pour se prosterner dans le temple du Style International. Dans le célèbre Seagram Building de Ludwig Mies van der Rohe, les architectes de génie Mies et Philip Johnson ont conçu dans les moindres détails la plus formidable salle de restaurant de Manhattan dans un grand souci de sobriété. Tout le reste, des sièges (Mies, Eero, Saarinen) aux flûtes de champagne (Garth et Ada Louise Huxtable), est l'œuvre de sommités du Modernisme. La cuisine contemporaine est à la hauteur du décor. Déjeuner au Grill Room est un rituel des grands de ce monde depuis son ouverture en 1959. John Kennedy y a fêté son 45ᵉ anniversaire en 1962.

Interior: The Pool Room by Philip Johnson has a Cararra marble pool in the center, and trees that "change" with the seasons. The Grill Room has an intriguing sculpture of bronze-colored rods by Richard Lippold.
Open: Mon–Fri midday–9:30pm (Sat from 11am); Sun closed. (jacket required, tie optional).
Prices: Lunch $ 38–65; dinner $ 39–150.
X-Factor: Guided tours Tue at 3pm.

Interieur: Im Pool Room von Philip Johnson steht ein riesiges Bassin aus Carrara-Marmor. Über der Bar im Grill Room hängt eine faszinierende Skulptur aus bronzefar-benen Stäben von Richard Lippold.
Öffnungszeiten: Mo–Fr 12–21.30 Uhr (Sa ab 11 Uhr); So geschlossen. (Jackett erforderlich, Schlips optional.)
Preise: Lunch 38–65 $; Dinner 39–150 $.
X-Faktor: Hausführungen dienstags um 15 Uhr.

Intérieur : La Pool Room de Philip Johnson possède un bassin central en marbre de Carrare. Dans le Grill Room, une intrigante sculpture en tiges couleur bronze de Richard Lippold trône au-dessus du bar.
Horaires d'ouverture : Lun–Ven 12h–21h30 (Sam à partir de 11h) ; Dim fermé. (Veste obligatoire, cravate optionelle.)
Prix : Déjeuner 38–65 $; dîner 39–150 $.
Le « petit plus » : Visites guidées le mardi à 15h.

Zibetto Espresso Bar

1385 6th Avenue, New York, NY 10019
☎ +1 646 707 0505
www.zibetto.com
Subway: 57th Street (F, N, Q, R, W)

When Zibetto's opened in midtown Manhattan in 2006, New York finally got its first serious Italian-style espresso bar. This is coffee for connoisseurs: Greek-Italian owner Anastasios Nougos trained at Stockholm's leading espresso bar, Sosta, and brought his expertise to New York – along with an affinity for Swedish design (his caffè is old-school traditional but the bar is sleek, white and modern.) There isn't any drip coffee here, and there aren't any seats either. As in Rome, you elbow your way to the bar, and grab the attention of the barista. He'll pull you a fresh shot of aromatic, smooth Zibetto-brand coffee. It's over in less than three minutes – but for those three minutes you've lived in coffee heaven.

Als Zibettos Espresso Bar 2006 in Midtown eröffnete, bekam New York endlich seine erste echt italienische Espresso-Bar. Hier gibt es Kaffee für Kenner: Der griechisch-italienisch-stämmige Besitzer Anastasios Nougos erlernte sein Handwerk im Sosta, der besten Espresso-Bar Stockholms, und brachte sein Wissen und seine Liebe zu schwedischem Design nach New York (der Kaffee ist traditionell, aber die Ausstattung ist schlicht, modern und weiß). Hier gibt es weder Filterkaffee noch Stühle: Stattdessen kämpft man sich wie in Rom zur Theke durch, erregt die Aufmerksamkeit der Barista und bekommt einen frisch und aromatisch zubereiteten Espresso der Traditionsmarke Zibetto – der Genuss dauert zwar nur drei Minuten, aber so lange ist man im Kaffee-Himmel.

Avec l'ouverture de Zibetto à Midtown en 2006, Manhattan a enfin eu son premier vrai bar à espresso italien. On y sert du café pour connaisseurs : le propriétaire gréco-italien, Anastasios Nougos, s'est formé au fameux Sosta de Stockholm. Il en a rapporté son savoir-faire ainsi qu'un penchant pour le design suédois (si le café est traditionnel, le bar est épuré, blanc et moderne). Ici, pas plus de cafetière électrique que de sièges. Comme à Rome, on joue des coudes jusqu'au comptoir où on attire l'attention du cafetier. Il vous servira un exprès aromatique, parfait et onctueux. Ça ne dure que trois minutes, mais trois minutes au paradis du café.

Interior: Clean, modern Scandinavian-style bar counter. Designed by Buster Delin.
Open: Mon–Fri 7am–7pm; Sat 9am–5pm; Sun 10am–4pm.
Prices: Espresso $ 2.50–3.50; cappuccino $ 4; panino $ 9.
X-Factor: The best espresso in New York.

Interieur: Geradlinig-moderne Theke im skandinavischen Stil. Design von Buster Delin.
Öffnungszeiten: Mo–Fr 7–19 Uhr; Sa 9–17 Uhr; So 10–16 Uhr.
Preise: Espresso 2,50–3,50 $; Cappuccino 4 $; Panino 9 $.
X-Faktor: Hier gibt es den besten Espresso in New York.

Intérieur : Clair, sobre et moderne à la Scandinave. Conçu par Buster Delin.
Horaires d'ouverture : Lun–Ven 7h–19h ; Sam 9h–17h ; Dim 10h–16h.
Prix : Espresso 2,50–3,50 $; capuccino 4 $; panino 9 $.
Le « petit plus » : Le meilleur espresso à New York.

Bergdorf Goodman BG Restaurant

754 5th Avenue, 7th Floor, New York, NY 10019
☎ +1 212 872 8977
www.bergdorfgoodman.com
Subway: 59th Street/5th Avenue (N, R, W), 57th Street (F)

The department store café, that venerable New York City institution, was stylishly re-invented in 2006, when Bergdorf Goodman's opened BG Restaurant, their new 7th-floor restaurant with breathtaking views of Central Park. The BG Restaurant was completely re-done for Bergdorf's by LA style guru Kelly Wearstler (designer of the Avalon Hotel in Beverly Hills, and Palm Springs' Viceroy). The four interconnected dining rooms are decorated in a whimsical American interpretation of classic European styles, with hand painted de Gournay chinoiserie wallpaper, and neo-Regency white chairs. Come to relax over coffee or tea or nibble a Lobster or Gotham Salad after a hectic day of shopping.

2006 wurde die ehrwürdige New Yorker Institution des Kaufhauscafés stilvoll und elegant neu erfunden, als Bergdorf Goodman auf der 7. Etage sein neues BG Restaurant mit weitem Blick über den Central Park eröffnete. L.A.-Stilguru Kelly Wearstler (Designerin des Avalon Hotels in Beverly Hills und des Viceroy in Palm Springs) hat das Restaurant völlig neu gestaltet. Die Ausstattung der vier verbundenen Speiseräume ist eine eigenwillige amerikanische Interpretation europäischen Stils mit handgedruckten Chinoiserie-Tapeten von de Gournay und weißen Neo-Regency-Stühlen. Hier kann man bei Kaffee oder Tee wunderbar entspannen oder nach einem hektischen Einkaufstag einen Hummer- oder Gotham-Salat genießen.

Le café du grand magasin Bergdorf Goodman, vénérable institution new-yorkaise, s'est refait une beauté en 2006. Kelly Wearstler, gourou du chic californien (elle a réalisé l'Avalon Hotel à Beverly Hills et le Viceroy à Palm Springs) s'est chargée de décorer les quatre salles du BG, situé au 7e étage, en réinterprétant avec espièglerie les grands styles d'Europe, optant pour des papiers peints en chinoiserie de chez de Gournay et des fauteuils blancs néo-Regency. Venez vous y détendre devant un café ou un thé, ou grignoter une salade de homard après une épuisante journée de shopping.

Interior: The "American Nouveau" design is by Los Angeles style guru Kelly Wearstler.
Open: Mon–Fri 11:30am– 8pm (Sat till 7pm); Sun midday–6pm; afternoon tea Mon–Sun 3pm–5pm.
Prices: Lunch, dinner $ 24–38.
X-Factor: Try to get one of the tables with a sweeping view of Central Park.

Interieur: Das „American Nouveau"-Design stammt von Kelly Wearstler, die auch die außergewöhnlichen Sessel entworfen hat.
Öffnungszeiten: Mo–Fr 11.30–20 Uhr (Sa bis 19 Uhr); So 12–18 Uhr; Nachmittagstee Mo–So 15–17 Uhr.
Preise: Lunch, Dinner 24–38 $.
X-Faktor: Man sollte versuchen, einen der wenigen Tische mit Blick über den Central Park zu ergattern.

Intérieur : Kelly Wearstler a conçu les intérieurs. Elle a aussi dessiné les bergères encapuchonnées.
Horaires d'ouverture : Lun–Ven 11h30– 20h (Sam jusqu'à 19h) ; Dim 12h–18h ; goûter Lun–Dim 15h–17h.
Prix : Déjeuner-dîner 24–38 $.
Le « petit plus » : Essayez d'obtenir une des quelques tables avec vue panoramique sur Central Park.

Bemelmans Bar

35 East 76th Street, New York, NY 10021
☎ +1 212 744 1600
www.thecarlyle.com
Subway: 77th Street (6)

The highlight of The Carlyle hotel's Bemelmans Bar is the magnificent mural that seems to wrap you in the sophisticated glow of another era. It was painted in 1947 by Austrian emigré artist Ludwig Bemelmans, creator of the children's book series, Madeline. He bartered his art work to The Carlyle in exchange for a year and a half free lodging at the swank hotel. His giddy, delightful images of a magical Central Park, complete with picnicking rabbits, will make you smile as you sip your old fashioned cocktail in this enclave of New York's "smart set".

Das Highlight der Bemelmans Bar im Carlyle Hotel ist das wunderbare Wandgemälde, das den Gast in eine andere Ära versetzt. Ludwig Bemelmans, österreichischer Auswanderer und Vater der Kinderbuchserie Madeline, schuf es 1947. Er tauschte seine Kunst gegen eineinhalb Jahre freies Logis in diesem prunkvollen Hotel. Seine fröhlichen und lustigen Bilder des magischen Central Parks – mitsamt Kaninchen beim Picknick – zaubern ein Lächeln auf das Gesicht der Gäste, die in dieser Enklave der eleganten Gesellschaft klassische Cocktails schlürfen.

Le grand attrait du Bemelmans Bar de l'hôtel Carlyle, c'est sa magnifique fresque qui vous enveloppe dans l'aura sophistiquée d'un autre temps. Elle fut peinte en 1947 par Ludwig Bemelmans, émigré autrichien et créateur de la série de livres pour enfants Madeline. Il avait troqué son travail contre un an et demi d'hébergement gratuit dans l'hôtel. Ses images charmantes d'un Central Park magique où pique-niquent des lapins vous raviront tandis que vous siroterez un cocktail dans cette enclave du New York huppé.

Interior: Glamorous, decadent mid-20th century, chocolate-brown leather banquettes, black glass tabletops, 24K gold leaf ceilings, updated in 2002 by Thierry Despont.
Open: Mon–Sun 12pm–12.30am.
Prices: Signature cocktails; bar snacks. Gin Gin Mule $ 20.
X-Factor: A jazz band plays music here every evening, so you can soak up the atmosphere of the 1940s.

Interieur: Schillernde Dekadenz mit braunen Lederbänken, schwarzen Glastischen und Decke aus 24-Karat-Blattgold, 2002 von Thierry Despont modernisiert.
Öffnungszeiten: Mo–So 12–0.30 Uhr.
Preise: Klassische Cocktails; Bar-Snacks. Gin Gin Mule 20 $.
X-Faktor: Jeden Abend spielt eine Jazzband Livemusik, sodass man hier in die Atmosphäre der 1940er eintauchen kann.

Intérieur : Style glamour avec banquettes en cuir chocolat, tables en verre fumé, plafonds dorés à la feuille ; rénové par Thierry Despont en 2002.
Horaires d'ouverture : Lun–Dim 12h–0.30h.
Prix : Cocktails classiques et en-cas. Gin Gin Mule 20 $.
Le « petit plus » : Un groupe de jazz joue ici tous les soirs et permet de retrouver l'atmosphère des années 1940.

E.A.T.

1064 Madison Avenue, New York, NY 10028
☎ +1 212 772 0022
www.elizabar.com/zabar
Subway: 77th Street (6), 86th Street (4, 5)

E.A.T. is Upper East Side Manhattan's answer to Hédiard in Paris or Harrods in London – it's where to go for unique gourmet salads, fish, appetizers and cold and hot meats. You can eat at a table in the simple café, or put together an elegant supper to take home. Alternatively get the Alpine picnic basket filled with good country bread, mountain cheeses, mustard and pickles and enjoy your meal in nearby Central Park. The owner, Eli Zabar, belongs to the famous Zabar delicatessen family – he broke away from the family lox, bagel and cheese business to start this more upscale, European-style emporium in 1973.

Das E.A.T. ist die Antwort der Upper East Side auf Hédiard in Paris oder Harrods in London. Hier findet man einzigartige Gourmetsalate, Fisch, Hors d'œuvres und kalte und warme Fleischwaren, die man entweder im schlichten Café genießen oder als elegantes Supper zum Mitnehmen zusammenstellen lassen kann. Als Alternative bietet sich der Alpin-Picknickkorb mit frischem Landbrot, Bergkäse, Senf und Pickles für einen Ausflug in den nahen Central Park an. Eigner Eli Zabar entstammt der berühmten Feinkost-Dynastie Zabar: 1973 kehrte er Lachs, Bagels und Käse den Rücken, um sein Luxuskaufhaus im europäischen Stil zu verwirklichen.

E.A.T. est la réponse du Upper East Side à l'Hédiard de Paris et au Harrods de Londres. On y vient pour ses petits plats cuisinés : salades, hors d'œuvres, poissons et viandes. Vous pouvez consommer sur place, assembler un dîner chic à emporter chez vous ou choisir un panier alpin garni de bon pain de campagne, de fromages de montagne, de moutarde et de pickles, et aller pique-niquer dans Central Park voisin. Le propriétaire, Eli Zabar, de la célèbre famille de traiteurs Zabar, a délaissé le saumon fumé et les bagels pour monter cette affaire plus haut de gamme à l'européenne en 1973.

Interior: Very 1980s – black-and-white tile floors, and butcher-block table tops, all designed by owner Eli Zabar.
Open: Mon–Sun 7am–10pm.
Prices: Sandwich plates $ 14.50–24; salads $ 10–20. Matzoh Ball Soup $ 10.
X-Factor: Eli Zabar's terrific custom-made Eastern European, French and Italian breads, rushed to E.A.T. from his nearby bakery which produces 40,000 pounds of bread daily.

Interieur: Typisch 1980er: schwarz-weißer Fliesenboden und Holztischplatten, von Eigner Eli Zabar selbst entworfen.
Öffnungszeiten: Mo–So 7–22 Uhr.
Preise: Sandwichteller 14,50–24 $; Salate 10–20 $. Matzoh Ball Soup 10 $.
X-Faktor: Eli Zabars großartige hausgemachte osteuropäische, französische und italienische Brote werden täglich von seiner nahe gelegenen Bäckerei angeliefert, die Tag für Tag etwa 20 Tonnen Brot produziert.

Intérieur : Très années 1980 : sols en damier, tables en billots de boucher, le tout conçu par le propriétaire Eli Zabar.
Horaires d'ouverture : Lun–Dim 7h–22h.
Prix : Assiette de sandwichs 14,40–24 $; salades 10–20 $. Matzoh Ball Soup 10 $.
Le « petit plus » : Les délicieux pains artisanaux français, italiens ou d'Europe de l'Est, tous frais sortis de la boulangerie d'Eli Zabar située à deux pas et qui produit près de 20 tonnes de pain par jour.

BASKETS

ELI'S FAMOUS THINS & CRISPS

E.A.T. COLLECTION

ELI'S SMOKED SALMON

ELI'S HANDMADE CHOCOLATES

THINS & CRISPS

HONEY PRETZELS

PALMIERS

CHOCOLATE BISCOTTI

PLAIN POTATO CHIPS

ELI'S NUTS

GIFT BASKETS

ELI'S HANDMADE CHOCOLATES

GIFT OF BREAD

EAT-TO-GO
PREPARED FOODS FOR PLANE, GIFT & HOME

SEAFOOD

POULTRY
Chicken Salad
Duck Salad
Grilled Chicken
Roast Chicken
w/ Carrots & Potatoes
Chicken in Whole Wine
Roast Turkey Wine
Roast Turkey Breast

MEATS

GALLEY

EGG & DAIRY

E.A.T.S

EXIT

I ♥ NY

Café Sabarsky

1048 5th Avenue, New York, NY 10028
☏ +1 212 288 0665
www.cafesabarsky.com
Subway: 86th Street (4, 5, 6)

In 2001, cosmetics mogul Ronald Lauder created a New York home for German and Austrian art when he opened the Neue Galerie in the Vanderbilt's old and sumptuous 5th Avenue mansion. But for many New Yorkers, the big attraction here isn't the breathtakingly expensive Klimts, but the delicious coffee and Apfelstrudel that awaits in the museum's Viennese Kaffeehaus. Austrian chef Kurt Gutenbrunner (also of Wallsé and Blaue Gans) is the mastermind behind Café Sabarsky, named in honor of art collector Serge Sabarsky, the museum's late co-founder. As you sip your perfect coffee at the round marble-top table, you'll forget you're in New York City. It's a perfect slice of Vienna.

2001 schuf der Kosmetik-Mogul Ronald Lauder mit der Neuen Galerie im alten und luxuriösen Vanderbilt-Haus an der Fifth Avenue eine Heimat für deutsche und österreichische Kunst. Für viele New Yorker sind aber nicht die atemberaubend teuren Klimts die Hauptattraktion, sondern der köstliche Kaffee und der Apfelstrudel im Wiener Kaffeehaus des Museums. Der Österreicher Kurt Gutenbrunner (der auch im Wallsé und in der Blauen Gans kocht) ist die treibende Kraft hinter dem Café Sabarsky, das nach dem verstorbenen Kunstsammler und Mitbegründer des Museums, Serge Sabarsky, benannt ist. Beim Kaffee an einem der runden Marmortische vergisst man fast, dass man sich in New York befindet – das Sabarsky ist ein perfektes Stück Wien.

En 2001, le magnat de l'industrie cosmétique Ronald Lauder a fondé la Neue Galerie dans le somptueux hôtel particulier des Vanderbilt sur la 5th Avenue afin d'y présenter l'art allemand et autrichien. Mais pour bon nombre de New-Yorkais, la grande attraction, ce ne sont pas les Klimt hors de prix mais les délicieux apfelstrudel du Kaffeehaus. Le chef autrichien Kurt Gutenbrunner (de Wallsé et Blaue Gans) est le maître d'œuvre derrière le Café Sabarsky, baptisé en l'honneur du cofondateur du musée, feu le collectionneur Serge Sabarsky. En dégustant son café parfait devant une petite table ronde en marbre, on se croirait à Vienne.

Interior: Grand period room inspired by the great fin-de-siècle Viennese cafés. Designed by Annabelle Selldorf, who also restored the magnificent Beaux-Arts 1914 mansion that houses the museum and café.
Open: Mon, Wed 9am–6pm; Thu–Sun 9am–9pm.
Prices: Breakfast $ 6–20; lunch, dinner $ 15–30.
X-Factor: The Café is also the site for the museum's many classical music concerts.

Interieur: Nobler, von Wiener Kaffeehäusern der Jahrhundertwende inspirierter Raum. Der Entwurf stammt von Annabelle Selldorf, die auch das Gebäude restaurierte, welches Museum und Café beherbergt.
Öffnungszeiten: Mo, Mi 9–18 Uhr; Do–So 9–21 Uhr.
Preise: Frühstück 6–20 $; Lunch, Dinner 15–30 $.
X-Faktor: Das Café ist auch Veranstaltungsort vieler klassischer Konzerte im Museum.

Intérieur : Salle grandiose inspirée par les grands cafés viennois de la fin du 19e siècle. Conçue par Annabelle Selldorf, qui a également restauré le magnifique hôtel particulier qui abrite le musée et le café.
Horaires d'ouverture : Lun, Mer 09h–18h ; Jeu–Dim 09h–21h.
Prix : Petit-déjeuner 6–20 $; déjeuner et dîner 15–30 $.
Le « petit plus » : Le café accueille de nombreux concerts de musique classique.

Rao's

455 East 114th Street, New York, NY 10029
☎ +1 212 722 6709
www.raos.com

Subway: 116th Street (6)

The ten tables in this Italian joint in Spanish Harlem are among the toughest reservations to get in New York. At Rao's tables are "owned" by a regular customer. Occasionally a spot opens up, but the wait can be months – or years. What makes Rao's hot is that its atmosphere is straight out of Sinatra's Rat Pack. Current owner Frank Pellegrino's nickname is "Frankie No" – because that is what he's usually telling would-be customers. With its aura of gangsters and wiseguys (Martin Scorsese cast several roles in Goodfellas with Rao's regulars), it's no wonder people would practically kill to eat Rao's famous meatballs with red sauce. But good luck. Bill Gates and Bill Clinton got in, but Madonna got turned away. The only Madonna at Rao's is their statue of the Virgin Mary.

Eine Reservierung in diesem italienischen Lokal in Spanish Harlem zählt zu den größten Herausforderungen in New York – denn hier „gehören" alle zehn Tische den Stammgästen. Ergibt sich mal eine Lücke in der Reservierungsliste, ist diese auf Monate oder Jahre ausgebucht. Was dieses Lokal zu einem begehrten Treffpunkt macht, ist seine Rat-Pack-Atmosphäre. Der Spitzname des Besitzers Frank Pellegrino lautet „Frankie No" – dank seiner Standardantwort an potenzielle Neukunden. Bei dieser Mafia-Atmosphäre verwundert es nicht, dass viele Leute für Rao's berühmte Fleischbällchen in Tomatensauce einen Mord begehen würden. Bill Gates und Bill Clinton haben hier Plätze bekommen, doch Madonna musste draußen bleiben.

Les dix tables de ce bistrot italien à Spanish Harlem ouvert en 1896 sont parmi les plus difficiles à obtenir car elles « appartiennent » aux habitués. Il arrive qu'un créneau se libère mais l'attente peut durer des mois, des années. Le grand attrait de Rao's, c'est son atmosphère très Rat Pack. Le propriétaire actuel, Frank Pellegrino (surnommé « Frankie No » à force de refuser les réservations) a interprété un rôle dans les Sopranos. Avec cette aura mafieuse (plusieurs habitués ont joué dans Les Affranchis), pas étonnant qu'on soit prêt à s'étriper pour déguster le célèbre poulet au citron ou les boulettes de viande en sauce rouge. Mais bonne chance : si Bill Gates et Bill Clinton sont entrés, Madonna attend toujours. La seule madone chez Rao's, c'est une statue de la Vierge.

Interior: Classic Italian-American living room – photos on the walls, tin ceiling, dark wood floor, jukebox in the corner, Christmas lights year-round.
Open: Mon–Fri 7pm–11pm. Without reservations – or an invite from a "regular" – fuggetaboutit.
Prices: Expensive, and cash only.
X-Factor: Their onlineshop sells their famous sauces, pastas and olive oils. There are online recipes, too.

Interieur: Klassische italienisch-amerikanische Wohnzimmeratmosphäre: Fotos, Holzböden. Jukebox in der Ecke und Weihnachtsbeleuchtung das ganze Jahr.
Öffnungszeiten: Mo–Fr 19–23 Uhr. Ohne Reservierung – oder Einladung eines Stammgastes – keine Chance.
Preise: Teuer – und nur Bares.
X-Faktor: Der Onlineshop, wo man die berühmten Saucen, Pasta und Olivenöle bestellen kann.

Intérieur : Restaurant italo-américain typique : photos aux murs, juke-box dans un coin, guirlandes de Noël toute l'année.
Horaires d'ouverture : Lun–Ven 19h–23h. Sans réservation ou l'invitation d'un « habitué », laissez tomber.
Prix : Cher et uniquement en espèces.
Le « petit plus » : Vous pouvez vous rendre sur leur site web pour acheter leurs célèbres sauces, leurs pâtes et leurs huiles d'olive. On y trouve aussi des recettes.

Shops

Jeffrey

Bergdorf
Goodman

Chelsea
Market

N

West Village
Tribeca
SoHo
Nolita
East Village
Lower East Side

Diane von Furstenberg
Jeffrey Ne[w] 10
Rick Owens
Murray's Cheese
Greenwich Letterpress
R 20th Century
Kiki de Montparnasse
TASCHEN
Jonathan Adler
Strand Book Store
Pearl River Mart
Opening Ceremony
MoMA Design Store SoHo
Dean & Deluca
Oak
BDDW
Kiehl's
Eileen's Cheesecake
Freemanns Sporting Club
Russ & Daughters

Hudson River Park
Washington Square Park
Tompkins Square Park
Seward Park
Hamilton Fish Park
Corlears Hook Park
East River Park
Governor Nelson A Rockefeller Park
Robert F Wagner Jr Park
North Cove
South Cove
Esplanade
City Hall Park
Thomas Paine Park
Park Row
Union Sq Park
Irving Pl
Stuyves Square

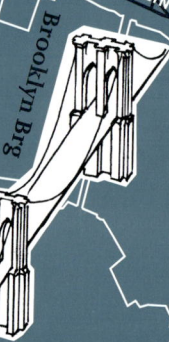

Brooklyn Brg
Manhattan Brg
Williamsburg Brg
Franklin D Roosevelt Dr
E River Piers

Bank St
Perry St
W 11th St
Morton St
Christopher St
Clarkson St
7TH AVE S
W 4th St
Waverly Place
W 12th St
W 13th St
W 14th St
W 15th St
W 16th St
Washington St
Hudson St
Varick St
6TH AVE
W 3rd St
Thompson St
W BROADWAY
Mercer St
Crosby St
Bleecker St
BROADWAY
LAFAYETTE ST
Prince St
Spring St
Kenmare St
Mott St
Mulberry St
Baxter St
BOWERY
Chrystie St
Eldridge St
ALLEN ST
Ludlow St
Essex St
Stanton St
Rivington St
Clinton St
E HOUSTON ST
Broome St
Grand St
Delancey St S
Avenue A
Avenue B
Avenue C
Avenue D
3RD AVE
2ND AVE
E 14TH ST
E 15th St
E 12th St
E 1 11th St
E 10th St
E 9th St
E 8th St
E 7th St
E 6th St
E 5th St
E 4th St
E 3rd St
E 2nd St
E 1st St

LAIGHT ST
CANAL ST
Beach St
N Moore St
Franklin St
Leonard St
White St
WALKER ST
Howard St
CENTRE ST
Worth St
Greenwich St
W Broadway
CHURCH ST
Duane St
Warren St
Murray St
Vesey St
N End Ave
Albany St
Liberty St
Chambers St
TRINITY PL
Nassau St
William St
Pearl St
ANN ST
FRANKFORT ST
PEARL ST
Front St
South St
STATE ST
Wall St
Battery Pl

Madison St
Cherry St
Henry St
Catherine St
E BROADWAY

Lincoln Tunnel

JOE DIMAGGIO HWY

Chelsea Waterside Park

12TH AVE

De Witt Clinton Park

11th Ave

11th Ave

W 42ND ST

W 43RD ST

W 44th St

W 45th St

W 46th St

W 47th St

W 48th St

W 49th St

W 50th St

W 51st St

W 52nd St

W 58th St

W 59th St

W 60th St

West End Ave

AMSTERDAM AVE

W 66TH ST

W 72ND ST

W 73rd St

W 74th St

W 75th St

W 76th St

W 77th St

W 78th St

W 79TH ST

10TH AVE

9TH AVE

9TH AVE

8TH AVE

W 53rd St

W 54th St

W 55th St

W 56TH ST

W 57TH ST

Hell's Kitchen

Midtown

W 65TH ST

W 64th St

W 67 th St

W 68th St

W 69th St

W 70th St

W 71st St

Chelsea

W 30TH ST

W 31st St

W 33rd St

W 34TH ST

W 35th St

W 36th St

W 37th St

W 38th St

W 39th St

W 40th St

BROADWAY

Columbus Circle

Park Dr S

IMAGINE

The Lake

TRANSVERSE RD

W 24th St

W 25th St

W 26th St

W 27th St

W 28th St

W 29th St

7th Ave

W 59TH ST

Central Park

65TH ST

6TH AVE

atiron

BROADWAY

Bryant Park

5th Ave

The Pond

Bergdorf Goodman

Apple Store

5th Ave

Madison Square Park

Tiffany & Co.

Madison Ave

J.Crew

Gramercy

PARK AVE S

Lexington Ave

Barneys New York

PARK AVE

Lexington Ave

Upper East Side

E 34TH ST

E 24th St

E 25th St

E 26th St

E 27th St

E 28th St

E 29th St

E 30th St

E 31st St

E 32nd St

E 33rd St

E 35th St

E 36th St

E 37th St

E 38th St

E 39th St

E 40th St

E 41st St

E 42ND ST

3RD AVE

3rd Ave

2ND AVE

2nd Ave

E 45th St

E 46th St

E 47th St

E 48th St

E 49th St

E 50th St

E 51st St

E 52nd St

E 53RD ST

E 54th St

E 55th St

E 56th St

E 57TH ST

E 58th St

E 59th St

E 60TH ST

E 61ST ST

E 62ND ST

E 63rd St

E 64th St

E 65TH ST

E 66TH ST

E 67th St

E 68th St

E 69th St

E 70th St

E 71st St

E 72ND ST

E 73rd St

E 74th St

E 75th St

E 76th St

E 77th St

E 78th St

E 79TH S

1ST AVE

1ST AVE

E River Dr

FDR DR

South Point Park

John Jay Park

Queensboro Brg

FDR DR

Newtown Creek

Dean & Deluca

560 Broadway, New York, NY 10012
☎ +1 212 226 6800
www.deandeluca.com

Subway: Prince Street (R, W), Broadway-Lafayette (B, D, F, V),
Spring Street (6)

Dean & Deluca has become an internationally known chain of fine food stores, but their original SoHo store is still the best. Joel Dean and Giorgio Deluca opened it as small gourmet grocery on the corner of Prince Street in 1977, the boom years of SoHo's art scene. Since then, the shop has expanded to over 10,000 square feet of glorious foods, spices, cookware, flowers, and exclusive chocolates from Christopher Norman and Fritz Knipschildt. It's all here: from a perfectly cut slice of jamón ibérico de bellota, to a wedge of truffled cheese from Umbria, to a bottle of Raz al Hanout from Morocco. Need a butcher? They've got an excellent one, as well as a fishmonger, bread bakery and patisserie.

Dean & Deluca hat sich zu einer international bekannten Feinkostkette entwickelt, doch das Stammhaus in SoHo ist immer noch ihr Flaggschiff. Joel Dean und Giorgio Deluca eröffneten es 1977, zur Boomzeit der Kunstszene in SoHo, als kleinen Delikatessenladen an der Ecke Prince Street. Seitdem wurde das Geschäft auf über 930 Quadratmeter erweitert und bietet exquisite Lebensmittel, Gewürze, Kochutensilien, Blumen und exklusive Pralinen von Christopher Norman und Fritz Knipschildt. Hier findet man alles, vom perfekt geschnittenen Jamón Ibérico de Bellota über getrüffelten Käse aus Umbrien bis zur Flasche Raz al Hanout aus Marokko. Und sonst? Dean & Deluca verfügt auch über eine exzellente Fleisch- und Fischabteilung sowie eine Bäckerei und Patisserie.

Dean & Deluca est mondialement connu comme une chaîne d'épiceries de luxe mais son fleuron reste sa première échoppe ouverte au coin de Prince Street en 1977, en plein boom artistique de SoHo. Elle s'est agrandie depuis et ses 930 mètres carrés sont remplis de délicieux produits, d'épices, d'ustensiles de cuisine, de fleurs et des divins chocolats de Christopher Norman et Fritz Knipschildt. Tout y est : du jambon ibérique bellota au fromage à la truffe d'Ombrie et à la bouteille de Raz al Hanout marocain. Il vous faut un boucher ? Il y en a un d'excellent, ainsi qu'un poissonnier, un boulanger et un pâtissier.

Interior: Located in a 19th century former warehouse. Artist and co-founder Jack Ceglic designed the original store with Carrara marble floors and white tile walls.
Open: Mon–Fri 7am–8pm (Sat–Sun from 8am).
X-Factor: Dean & Deluca's stand-up coffee bar is a great place to grab a quick espresso and a scone or a bagel – eat them at the steel counter by the window, and enjoy the best people-watching spot in SoHo.

Interieur: Ein ehemaliges Lagerhaus aus dem 19. Jahrhundert. Künstler und Mitbegründer Jack Ceglic hat das Stammhaus mit Böden aus Carrara-Marmor und weiß gefliesten Wänden entworfen.
Öffnungszeiten: Mo–Fr 7–20 Uhr (Sa–So ab 8 Uhr).
X-Faktor: Das Stehcafé Dean & Deluca ist perfekt für einen schnellen Espresso, und die Theke am Fenster ist der beste Platz zum Sehen und Gesehenwerden in ganz SoHo.

Intérieur : Situé dans un ancien entrepôt du 19ᵉ siècle. L'artiste et cofondateur Jack Ceglic l'a aménagé avec des sols en marbre de Carrare et des murs en carrelage blanc.
Horaires d'ouverture : Lun–Ven 7h–20h (Sam–Dim à partir de 8h).
Le « petit plus » : Commandez un café avec un bagel ou un scone et consommez-les debout au comptoir en acier devant la fenêtre pour contempler le défilé haut en couleur des habitants de SoHo.

Opening Ceremony

33–35 Howard Street, New York, NY 10013
☎ +1 212 219 2688
www.openingceremony.us
Subway: Canal Street (N, Q, R, W, 6, J, M, Z)

Opening Ceremony, which takes its name from the Olympics, is a truly global fashion store. In 2002, owners Carol Lim and Humberto Leon came up with a unique concept: every year they travel to a different country, immerse themselves in the culture and fashion, and return here with one-of-a-kind clothes, shoes and accessories from designers, artisans, even from open-air markets. So far they've "done" Hong Kong, Brazil, Germany, the U.K., Sweden, Japan, France, Argentina, Korea, and Belgium. Designers and labels include Proenza Schouler, Alexander Wang, Rodarte, Chloë Sevigny, and Band of Outsiders.

Opening Ceremony, nach der Eröffnungsfeier der Olympischen Spiele benannt, ist wirklich international. 2002 hatten Carol Lim und Humberto Leon die originelle Idee, jedes Jahr in ein fremdes Land zu reisen, dessen Kultur und Mode zu erkunden und mit einer Auswahl einzigartiger Kleider, Schuhe und Accessoires von Designern, Kunsthandwerkern, aber auch von Flohmärkten zurückzukehren. Bisher haben sie Hongkong, Brasilien, Deutschland, Großbritannien und Nordirland, Schweden, Japan, Frankreich, Argentinien, Korea und Belgien bereist. Zu ihren Designern und Marken zählen Proenza Schouler, Alexander Wang, Rodarte, Chloë Sevigny und Band of Outsiders.

Tirant son nom de la cérémonie d'ouverture des Jeux Olympiques, voici une boutique vraiment planétaire. En 2002, Carol Lim et Humberto Leo ont inventé un nouveau concept : chaque année, il se rendent dans un pays différent, s'immergent dans sa culture et sa mode puis en reviennent avec des vêtements, des chaussures et des accessoires de stylistes, d'artisans et même de marchés locaux. Ils ont déjà « fait » Hong Kong, le Brésil, l'Allemagne, la Grande-Bretagne, la Suède, le Japon, la France, l'Argentine, la Corée et la Belgique. Leurs stylistes et leurs marques incluent Proenza Schouler, Alexander Wang, Rodarte, Chloë Sevigny et Band of Outsiders.

Interior: The factory space was a former Pond's Cold Cream Factory; new interiors designed by Harry Lee and Shannon Han.
Open: Mon–Sat 11am–8pm; Sun midday–7pm.
X-Factor: Most of what you'll find here is exclusive; almost all the designers represented at Opening Ceremony launched their careers at the store.

Interieur: In den Räumlichkeiten befand sich früher eine Fabrik, in der die berühmte Pond's Cold Cream produziert wurde; die neue Inneneinrichtung stammt von Harry Lee und Shannon Han.
Öffnungszeiten: Mo–Sa 11–20 Uhr; So 12–19 Uhr.
X-Faktor: Fast alles, was man hier findet, ist exklusiv, und die Karriere vieler der bei Opening Ceremony vertretenen Designer hat genau hier begonnen.

Intérieur : L'espace industriel abritait autrefois une usine de crème de beauté Pond ; les nouveaux intérieurs ont été créés par Harry Lee et Shannon Han.
Horaires d'ouverture : Lun–Sam 11h–20h ; Dim 12h–19h.
Le « petit plus » : Presque tout ce que vous trouverez dans cette boutique est exclusif. Pratiquement tous les stylistes représentés ont débuté leur carrière ici.

OPENING CEREMONY Est. 2002

BDDW

---

5 Crosby Street, New York, NY 10013
☎ +1 212 625 1230
www.bddw.com
Subway: Canal Street (N, Q, R, W, 6)

This is an absolute must for anyone who loves the feel and look of hand-finished wood. American painter and sculptor Tyler Hays's beds, chairs, tables, stools and mirrors have a serene, Shaker-like simplicity. Every piece is hand made in BDDW's Philadelphia, Pennsylvania workshop and beautifully hand finished by rubbing with oil. This 7,000-square-foot showroom, opened in 2002, is the one and only BDDW outlet in the US and a visit on every trip to New York is always a joyful experience.

Ein absolutes Muss für jeden, der Aussehen und Haptik von handbearbeitetem Holz liebt. Die Betten, Stühle, Tische, Hocker und Spiegel des amerikanischen Malers und Bildhauers Tyler Hays bestechen durch ihre gelassene, an Shaker-Möbel erinnernde Schlichtheit. Alle Stücke werden in der Werkstatt in Philadelphia (Pennsylvania) von Hand gefertigt und abschließend geölt. Die im Jahr 2002 eröffnete, 650 Quadratmeter große Verkaufsfläche ist die einzige Vertriebsstelle von BDDW und lohnt in den USA unbedingt einen Besuch.

Un must pour tous les amateurs d'ébénisterie. Les lits, chaises, tables, tabourets et miroirs du peintre et sculpteur américain Tyler Hays ont une simplicité sereine qui rappelle le mobilier Shaker. Toutes les pièces sont réalisées à la main dans l'atelier de BDDW à Philadelphie, Pennsylvanie, et frottées à l'huile pour une finition parfaite. Ce showroom de 650 mètres carrés, ouvert en 2002, est le seul de BDDW aux États-Unis et mérite une visite à chaque séjour à New York.

Interior: Located in a 19th-century SoHo carriage house with 14-foot-high brick arches throughout. Paintings are by Tyler Hays, who also designed the space.
Open: Mon–Fri 10am–6pm; Sat midday–6pm.
X-Factor: BDDW's best selling "Flower Bed" has a flower inlay in the headboard, and a secret, built-in drawer for all the things you want to hide under your bed.

Interieur: In einem SoHoer Kutschhaus aus dem 19. Jahrhundert mit 4,30 Meter hohen Backsteinbögen untergebracht. Gemälde und Innenarchitektur stammen von Tyler Hays.
Öffnungszeiten: Mo–Fr 10–18 Uhr; Sa 12–18 Uhr.
X-Faktor: BDDWs Verkaufshit „Flower Bed" bietet eine Blumen-Intarsie im Kopfteil und eine verborgene Schublade für all die Dinge, die man gern unter dem Bett versteckt.

Intérieur : Ancien hangar à voitures du 19e siècle à SoHo, avec des voûtes en brique de 4,30 mètres de haut. Les tableaux sont de Tyler Hays, qui a aménagé l'espace.
Horaires d'ouverture : Lun–Ven 10h–18h ; Sam 12h–18h.
Le « petit plus » : Le « Flower Bed », le meuble que BDDW vend le plus, a une tête de lit ornée d'une fleur en marqueterie et un tiroir « secret » pour tout ce que vous voulez cacher sous votre matelas.

Pearl River Mart

477 Broadway, New York, NY 10013
☎ +1 212 431 4770
www.pearlriver.com
Subway: Canal Street (N, Q, R, W), Spring Street (6)

Pearl River Mart sells everyday items from Mainland China. In the 1970s, it became a must-stop for a downtown artsy clientele eager for kung-fu black cotton slippers and blue Mao suits, and farmer's umbrellas made from bamboo and waxed rice-paper. The big new store in SoHo opened in 2004, and it's stuffed with both kitsch and Chinese treasures – silk brocaded slippers, robes and pajamas, vases and ceramics, paper lanterns. Be sure to check out the basement for their cheap, beautiful silk thermal underwear.

Pearl River Mart verkauft alles, was aus China kommt. In den 1970er-Jahren entwickelte sich das Geschäft an der Canal Street bei der Downtown-Kunstszene, die auf schwarze Kung-Fu-Latschen, blaue Mao-Anzüge und Bauernschirme aus Bambus und gewachstem Reispapier stand, zum absoluten Muss. Der neue Laden öffnete 2004 in SoHo seine Pforten und ist vollgestopft mit Kitsch und echten Schätzen – von bestickten Seidenpantoffeln, Kimonos und Pyjamas über Vasen und Keramiken bis zu Lampions. Vor allem die preiswerte Thermo-Seidenunterwäsche im Untergeschoss sollte man sich nicht entgehen lassen oder das schlichte blau-weiße Geschirr aus Japan, das in jeder Wohnung gut aussieht.

Le Pearl River Mart vend des articles de Chine. Dans les années 1970, c'était le temple des bobos en quête de chaussons de kung-fu en coton noir, de costumes Mao bleus et d'ombrelles de paysan en bambou et papier de riz ciré. La nouvelle grande boutique de SoHo, inaugurée en 2004, est remplie de kitscheries et de trésors : pantoufles, robes de chambre et pyjamas en brocard de soie, vases et céramiques, lanternes en papier… Ne ratez pas le sous-sol, avec ses sous-vêtements en soie Thermolactyl beaux et bon marché.

Interior: The building is a converted former SoHo fabric warehouse – loft-like space with high ceilings and wood floors.
Open: Mon–Sun 10am–7:20pm.
X-Factor: This is where smart New Yorkers come to shop for unique, unusual and pocket-friendly gifts.

Interieur: Das loftartige Gebäude mit hohen Decken und Holzböden war früher ein Lagerhaus für Stoffe.
Öffnungszeiten: Mo–So 10–19.20 Uhr.
X-Faktor: Hierher kommt der smarte New Yorker, um ausgefallene, einzigartige und geldbeutelschonende Geschenke zu kaufen.

Intérieur : Ancien entrepôt de tissus reconverti. Grand espace ouvert avec hauts plafonds et parquet.
Horaires d'ouverture : Lun–Dim 10h–19h20.
Le « petit plus » : C'est ici que les New-Yorkais malins viennent acheter des cadeaux uniques et originaux sans se ruiner.

Jonathan Adler

53 Greene Street, New York, NY 10013
☎ +1 212 941 8950
www.jonathanadler.com
Subway: Canal Street (A, C, E, N, Q, R, W)

"We believe minimalism is a bummer." That maxim, from the manifesto of designer extraordinaire Jonathan Adler (he did the Parker Palm Springs hotel) makes a fitting introduction to his giddy 2,200-square-foot SoHo home decor store. Opened in 1998, just after Adler gained fame for his Barneys New York collection of irreverent, 1960s-style pottery (Adler is married to Barneys Creative Ambassador at Large Simon Doonan), this is where you can find all his fun and very groovy furniture, decor, rugs, pillows, bedding, lighting and fashion accessories for men, women, and children.

„Wir finden: Minimalismus ist Mist." Diese Maxime des Ausnahmedesigners Jonathan Adler (er gestaltete z. B. das Hotel Parker Palm Springs) ist die perfekte Beschreibung für sein 205 Quadratmeter großes Einrichtungshaus in SoHo. Es wurde 1998 eröffnet, kurz nachdem Adler für seine respektlose Keramikserie im 1960er-Jahre-Stil für Barneys New York (mit dessen Creative Ambassador at Large Simon Doonan er verheiratet ist) viel gerühmt wurde. Hier kann man Adlers lustige und fetzige Möbel bewundern, seine Dekors, Teppiche, Kissen, Bettwaren, Lampen und Modeaccessoires für Damen, Herren und Kinder.

« Le minimalisme, c'est l'ennui. » Cette devise, extraite du manifeste du designer Jonathan Adler (décorateur de l'hôtel Parker Palm Springs) convient parfaitement à son immense boutique de décoration de 205 mètres carrés à SoHo. Ouverte en 1998, juste après qu'il se soit illustré avec sa ligne de céramiques irrévérencieuses très « années soixante » pour Barneys (il est marié à l'ambassadeur artistique de Barneys, Simon Doonan), on y trouve des meubles plein d'humour, de la déco, des couvertures, des coussins, de la literie, mais aussi des accessoires d'éclairage et de mode pour hommes, femmes et enfants.

Interior: Designed by Jonathan Adler, the shop, in an old SoHo industrial building, looks like a cross between Austin Powers' pad and your grandmother's Palm Beach summer house.
Open: Mon–Sat 11am–7pm; Sun midday–6pm.
X-Factor: The hashish candle and king-and-queen mugs inspired by Bjørn Wiinblad are among the most special and nicest souvenirs you can bring from New York.

Interieur: Das Ladenlokal in einem Industriegebäude wirkt wie eine Kreuzung aus Austin Power's Junggesellenbude und Großmutters Sommerhaus in Palm Beach.
Öffnungszeiten: Mo–Sa 11–19 Uhr; So 12–18 Uhr.
X-Faktor: Die Haschischkerze und die von Bjørn Wiinblad inspirierten King- und Queen-Becher zählen zu den ausgefallensten und nettesten Souvenirs, die man in New York kaufen kann.

Intérieur : Conçue par Jonathan Adler dans un vieil immeuble industriel de SoHo, la boutique ressemble à un croisement entre la garçonnière d'Austin Powers et la maison d'été de votre grand-mère à Palm Beach.
Horaires d'ouverture : Lun–Sam 11h–17h ; Dim 12h–18h.
Le « petit plus » : La bougie au haschich et les tasses du roi et de la reine inspirées par Bjørn Wiinblad sont des souvenirs sympathiques et originaux de New York.

NTER OUR groovyworld

Kiki de Montparnasse

79 Greene Street, New York, NY 10012
☎ +1 212 965 8150
www.kikidm.com
Subway: Prince Street (R, W), Spring Street (6)

This luxury boutique in SoHo offers an elegant, immersive experience of indulgence and discovery. The store suggests a lavish salon with vintage and custom modern furniture and a renowned fine art collection including works by Helmut Newton, Thomas Ruff, and Araki. Its sumptuous velvet dressing rooms with customizable lighting settings are a magical space for lovers and friends. Sophisticated and sensual ready-to-wear, lounge and lingerie collections; fashion accessories; fine jewelry; home, fragrance, bath and body lines — all reflect refined and timeless design aesthetics and are handcrafted from the highest quality materials.

In diese elegante Luxusboutique in SoHo kann man eintauchen, sich wohlfühlen und auf Endeckungsreise gehen. Der Laden erinnert an einen noblen Salon mit antikem wie eigens angefertigtem modernem Mobiliar und einer renommierten Kunstsammmlung mit Werken von Helmut Newton, Thomas Ruff, Araki und anderen. Die luxuriösen samtverkleideten Anproben mit individuell anpassbarer Beleuchtung sind ein magischer Ort für Freunde und Liebhaber. Raffinierte und sinnliche Kollektionen mit Prêt-à-porter, Alltagskleidung und Dessous, Modeaccessoires, edler Schmuck, Düfte sowie Produkte rund ums Haus, für Bad und Körper — all dies spiegelt eine kultivierte und zeitlose Design-Ästhetik, rundum handgearbeitet aus hochwertigsten Materialien.

Cette boutique de dessous de luxe à SoHo invite à une promenade passion-nante au cœur de l'élégance. Son salon richement décoré présente dans un ameublement vintage moderne une collection d'art renommée incluant des œuvres d'Helmut Newton, Thomas Ruff et Araki. Ses somptueuses salles d'essayage tendues de velours aux éléments lumineux intégrés est un endroit magique pour amoureux et amis. Le prêt-à-porter sophistiqué et sensuel, les collections de lingerie, les accessoires de mode, les bijoux raffinés, les produits de bain et parfums — tout reflète une esthétique de design subtile et indémodable élaborée à partir de matériaux haut de gamme.

Interior: The building is located in SoHo's historic Cast-Iron District; the spare, elegant black-and-white interior is by Commune
Open: Tue–Sat 11am–8pm (Sun–Mon till 7 pm).
X-Factor: The Boutique is the exclusive outlet for E.R. Butler & Co.'s "Pearl Restraints" — ten feet of freshwater pearls. A classic erotic symbol.

Interieur: Das Gebäude liegt in SoHos historischem Cast-Iron District; der weitläufige, elegante Innenraum stammt von Commune.
Öffnungszeiten: Di–Sa 11–20 Uhr (So–Mo bis 19 Uhr).
X-Faktor: Die Boutique ist alleiniger Verkäufer für die "Pearl Restraints" von E.R. Butler & Co., von Hand auf drei Meter lange Schnüre aufgezogene Ketten aus Süßwasserperlen — ein klassisches erotisches Symbol.

Intérieur : Située dans le « quartier de la fonte » à SoHo, l'élégante boutique a été décorée par Commune.
Horaires d'ouverture : Mar–Sam 11h–20h (Dim–Lun jusqu'à 19h).
Le « petit plus » : La bouique a l'exclusivité des « liens de perles » de E. R. Butler & Co : des rangs de perles de trois mètres de long. Symbole érotique traditionnel, les perles enfilées à la main sont conçues comme parure élégante et inspiration sensuelle.

MoMA Design Store SoHo

81 Spring Street, New York, NY 10012
☎ +1 646 613 1367
www.momastore.org
Subway: Prince Street (R, W), Spring Street (6)

This downtown branch of The Museum of Modern Art's popular shop opened in 2001. Here you'll find 3,300 square feet of high-end design objects – pens, scarves, desk accessories, furniture, watches and even household items like brooms by noted designers old and new: Philippe Starck, Massimo Vignelli, Verner Panton, Achille Castiglioni. Every product sold here is approved by a MoMA curator. Explore their newly expanded children's section and their Muji for MoMA collection, featuring the store's best selling gift item, "New York City in a Bag".

Der Downtown-Ableger des beliebten Shops im Museum of Modern Art eröffnete 2001 und bietet auf 307 Quadratmetern hochwertige Design-objekte wie Stifte, Schals, Schreib-tischaccessoires, Möbel, Uhren und sogar Haushaltsgegenstände von De-signern wie Philippe Starck, Massimo Vignelli, Verner Panton oder Achille Castiglioni. Jeder hier verkaufte Ge-genstand wurde von einem MoMA-Kurator abgesegnet. Entdecken Sie die kürzlich erweiterte Kinderabteilung sowie die Sammlung "Muji for Mo-MA" mit dem begehrtesten Geschenk-artikel des Ladens: „New York City in a Bag".

Cette annexe de 307 mètres carrés de la boutique du Museum of Modern Art a ouvert à Downtown en 2001. On y trouve des objets design haut de gamme : stylos, écharpes, accessoires de bureau, meubles, montres et même des ustensiles de ménage dont des balais signés de grands créateurs tels que Philippe Starck, Massimo Vignelli, Verner Panton ou Achille Castiglioni. Tous les articles sont approuvés par le conservateur du MoMA. Explorez le rayon enfants récemment agrandi et le stand Muji pour la collection de MoMA, présentant le produit le plus vendu du magasin : « New York dans un sac ».

Interior: Renovated landmark SoHo cast-iron building. The two-level, open-plan inte-rior was designed by 1100 Architect.
Open: Mon–Sat 10am–8pm; Sun 11am–7pm.
X-Factor: All purchases support the exhibi-tions and programs of The Museum of Mod-ern Art.

Interieur: Saniertes Wahrzeichen von SoHo. Die zweigeschossigen, offen gestalteten Verkaufsräume wurden von 1100 Architects entworfen.
Öffnungszeiten: Mo–Sa 10–20 Uhr; So 11–19 Uhr.
X-Faktor: Mit dem Verkauf werden die Aus-stellungen und Projekte des Museum of Modern Art unterstützt.

Intérieur : Situé dans un ancien immeuble en fonte à SoHo. Les deux niveaux de type loft ont été aménagés par 1100 Architect.
Horaires d'ouverture : Lun–Sam 10h–20h ; Dim 11h–19h.
Le « petit plus » : Les bénéfices financent en partie les expositions et programmes du MoMA.

Staff Picks
New York and Travel
Gift Books
PIANO
CALATRAVA
MODERNISM REDISCOVERED
Architecture
HOUSES
CARS
BEGUILED BY THE WILD
LET'S WRESTLE
-ISMS AND -OLOGIES
LOOK
ARCHITECTURAL wonders
ReadyMade
NEW YORK
New York
THE LIGHT OF NEW YORK
THE ELEMENTS OF STYLE

TASCHEN

107 Greene Street, New York, NY 10012
☎ +1 212 226 2212
www.taschen.com
Subway: Prince Street (R, W)

Beautiful books deserve a beautiful setting, and so TASCHEN created the New York outpost, opened in 2006, with an eye towards maximizing the aesthetic experience – and the fun. Here you can relax in a comfy chair by Arne Jacobsen and browse through the pages of The Big Penis Book, or another of the offerings, surrounded by the bubbly, psychedelic floor-to-ceiling murals by Brazilian artist Beatriz Milhazes, and by bookshelves that seem to float weightlessly in the air. There's something for everyone here, whether you are interested in art, architecture, travel or erotica, and no matter if your budget is 7.99 or 15,000 dollars.

Schöne Bücher verdienen eine schöne Umgebung – deshalb konzipierte TASCHEN seine 2006 eröffnete New Yorker Filiale mit Blick auf eine Maximierung des ästhetischen Erlebnisses. Allerdings sollte auch der Spaß beim Einkaufen nicht zu kurz kommen! Hier können Sie sich in einem behaglichen Sessel von Arne Jacobsen niederlassen und entspannt in The Big Penis Book oder anderen Angeboten blättern – umgeben von übersprudelnden, psychedelischen, deckenhohen Wandgemälden der brasilianischen Künstlerin Beatriz Milhazes und Bücherregalen, die schwerelos in der Luft zu schweben scheinen. Bei TASCHEN findet sich etwas für jeden Geschmack und jeden Geldbeutel – von Kunst über Architektur und Reisen bis hin zu Erotika und zwar von 7,99 bis 15.000 Dollar.

Les beaux livres méritent un décor d'exception. TASCHEN a ouvert sa boutique new-yorkaise en 2006 avec la ferme intention d'en faire une expérience esthétique et de plaisir. Confortablement installé dans un fauteuil d'Arne Jacobsen, vous pouvez feuilleter The Big Penis Book entouré par les fresques psychédéliques de la brésilienne Beatriz Milhazes et d'étagères qui semblent flotter. Il y en a pour tous les goûts, que vous vous intéressiez à l'art, à l'architecture, aux voyages ou à l'érotisme, que votre budget soit de 7,99 ou de 15 000 dollars.

Interior: Historic SoHo cast-iron building, interior designed by Philippe Starck.
Open: Mon–Sat 11am–7pm; Sun midday–7pm.
X-Factor: Check out the downstairs gallery for special book-signing events, plus exhibits of photographs by Julius Shulman, and an original suite by Brazilian designer Sergio Rodrigues.

Interieur: Historisches Cast-Iron-Gebäude in SoHo, Raumgestaltung von Philippe Starck.
Öffnungszeiten: Mo–Sa 11–19 Uhr; So 12–19 Uhr.
X-Faktor: Im Untergeschoss finden regelmäßig Signierstunden statt; außerdem erwarten den Besucher hier eine Ausstellung mit Fotografien von Julius Shulman und eine Möbelgarnitur des brasilianischen Designers Sergio Rodrigues.

Intérieur : Immeuble en fonte classé à SoHo. Décor conçu par Philippe Starck.
Horaires d'ouverture : Lun–Sam 11h–19h ; Dim 12h–19h.
Le « petit plus » : Dans la galerie en sous-sol, qui accueille une suite originale du designer brésilien Sergio Rodrigues, sont organisées des séances de signatures et des expositions de photographes tel que Julius Shulman.

Rick Owens

250 Hudson Street, New York, NY 10013
☎ +1 212 627 7222
www.rickowens.eu

Subway: Spring Street (C, E), Canal Street (1)

This California-born, Paris-based designer certainly understands showmanship. He opened his first New York boutique in 2008 in an area between SoHo and Tribeca, which was one of the last empty corners of Manhattan. The store has put the neighborhood on the map. Fashionistas as well as celebrity Owens fans like Julianne Moore have their limos waiting at the curb. They come, of course, for Owens' beautifully cut, post-punk Goth creations in soft leathers and cashmeres – and also to marvel at his store's most unusual attraction: a "fog aquarium" installation. Every few minutes, a wall of steam whirls up behind the sales counter, to mesmerizing theatrical effect.

Dieser aus Kalifornien stammende, inzwischen aber in Paris ansässige Designer versteht es wahrlich, sich in Szene zu setzen: 2008 öffnete er seine erste New Yorker Boutique in einer Ecke zwischen SoHo und Tribeca – einem der letzten nicht überlaufenen Viertel Manhattans, das jedoch durch die Eröffnung in den Mittelpunkt des Interesses rückte. Fashionistas und prominente Fans des Designers wie Julianne Moore geben sich hier die Klinke in die Hand, auf der Suche nach Owens' wundervoll geschnittenen, Post-Punk-Goth-Kreationen aus weichem Leder und Kaschmir. Eine weitere Attraktion ist Owens' „Nebel-Aquarium" – eine Installation direkt hinter der Ladentheke, aus der alle paar Minuten Wirbel aus Dampfschwaden aufsteigen und die Kundschaft in ihren Bann schlagen.

Ce styliste californien basé à Paris a le sens de la mise en scène. En ouvrant en 2008 sa première boutique new-yorkaise dans le dernier recoin désert de Manhattan, entre SoHo et Tribeca, il a révélé un nouveau quartier. Les limousines de célébrités comme Julianne Moore attendent devant la porte. On y vient naturellement pour les créations post-punk gothiques impeccablement taillées en cuir et cachemire mais également pour admirer l'« aquarium de brouillard ». À intervalles réguliers, des volutes de vapeur théâtrales et hypnotiques s'enroulent derrière une vitre derrière le comptoir de vente.

Interior: The high-ceiling white space with towering six-way mirror was designed by Rick Owens.
Open: Mon–Fri 11am–7pm; Sat midday–7pm; Sun midday–6pm.
X-Factor: The curvy, sculptural wooden chairs and benches in the store were also designed by Rick Owens – they're part of his furniture collection sold through the Carpenters Workshop Gallery in London.

Interieur: Der weiße Raum mit den hohen Decken und dem hoch aufragenden sechsteiligen Spiegel wurde von Rick Owens persönlich entworfen.
Öffnungszeiten: Mo–Fr 11–19 Uhr; Sa 12–19 Uhr; So 12–18 Uhr.
X-Faktor: Die geschwungenen, skulpturalen Sitzmöbel und Bänke aus Holz stammen ebenfalls von Rick Owens – sie sind Teil seiner Möbelkollektion und über die Carpenters Workshop Gallery in London erhältlich.

Intérieur : L'espace blanc haut de plafond avec d'immenses miroirs à six faces a été conçu par Rick Owens.
Horaires d'ouverture : Lun–Ven 11h–19h ; Sam midi–19h ; Dim midi–18h.
Le « petit plus » : Les chaises et les bancs sculpturaux en bois ont été dessinés par Rick Owens. Ils font partie de sa ligne de mobilier vendue parla Carpenters Workshop Gallery à Londres.

Murray's Cheese

254 Bleecker Street, New York, NY 10014
☎ +1 212 243 3289
www.murrayscheese.com

Subway: West 4th Street (A, C, E, F, V),
West 4th Street-Washington Square (B, D)

New York's oldest and most famous cheese shop opened in 1940. It's been through a few moves (it used to be in a much smaller place across the street) and management changes, but one thing hasn't changed: the cheese selection is the best and most comprehensive in the city. The variety here is head-spinning – from rare Spanish manchegos, Neal's Yard Dairy, to artisan goat cheese from small, local American farms. Murray's also has its own cheese caves and classrooms where they offer daily classes and tastings.

New Yorks ältester und bekanntester Käseladen besteht bereits seit 1940. Er hat so manchen Wandel (früher war er in einem viel kleineren Lokal gegenüber) und Wechsel in der Geschäftsleitung erlebt, aber die Käseauswahl ist weiterhin die beste und umfangreichste der Stadt. Die atemberaubende Vielfalt reicht von seltenen spanischen Manchegos über Produkte von Neal's Yard Dairy bis zu Ziegenkäse von kleinen amerikanischen Käsereien. Murray's hat auch einen eigenen Käsekeller zum Reifen der Käse sowie Unterrichtszimmer, in denen Verkostungen und Lehrgänge stattfinden.

Le fromager le plus ancien et le plus célèbre de New York a ouvert en 1940. Il a connu quelques changements de direction et de lieu (il occupait un espace plus petit en face) mais une chose est restée immuable : la sélection de fromages la plus complète et la meilleure de la ville. Le choix est étourdissant, des manchegos rares espagnols aux produits de Neal's Yard en passant par les chèvres artisanaux de petits producteurs américains. Murray possède aussi ses propres caves à fromages et des salles de classes où sont proposés des dégustations et des cours quotidiens.

Interior: Classic New York deli. State-of-the-art cheese caves.
Open: Mon–Sat 8am–8pm; Sun 10am–7pm.
X-Factor: Head three doors down to Murray's Cheese Bar (264 Bleecker Street), where the homage to fromage continues with delicious cheese plates, artisan wines and craft beers, as well as mac and cheese, cheeseburgers, pastas, and salads.

Interieur: Klassisches New Yorker Deli. Moderne Käsegewölbe.
Öffnungszeiten: Mo–Sa 8–20 Uhr; So 10–19 Uhr.
X-Faktor: Drei Türen weiter gibt es Murray's Cheese Bar (264 Bleecker Street), wo die Hommage an den fromage weitergeht mit leckeren Käseplatten, handwerklich hergestellten Weinen und Bieren sowie Makkaroni und Käse, Cheeseburger, Pasta und Salat.

Intérieur : Caves à fromage haut de gamme.
Horaires d'ouverture : Lun–Sam 8h–20h ; Dim 10h–19h.
Le « petit plus » : Allez trois portes plus loin au Murray's Cheese Bar (264 Bleecker Street) où l'hommage rendu au fromage se poursuit en de délicieux plats de fromages, vins et bières artisanaux, sans oublier les macaronis au fromage, les cheeseburgers, les pâtes et les salades.

DELICATE
TOASTY
BITING Nutty
Crumbly DECADENT
FARMSTEAD
&
Pervasive SUBTLE
LINGERING
AGED
MEAT
MONS
98
Brunet
YELLOW CHEDDAR
$5.99lb
JARLSBERG
$9.99lb
$15.99lb
JALAPENO JACK
LE GRUYERE
IRISH CHEDDAR

Greenwich Letterpress

39 Christopher Street, New York, NY 10014
☎ +1 212 989 7464
www.greenwichletterpress.com

Subway: Christopher Street-Sheridan Square (1),
West 4th Street (A, C, E, F, V),
West 4th Street-Washington Square (B, D)

Beth and Amy Salvini come from a family that has been in the printing business for three generations. The sisters opened this tiny shop on Christopher Street in the West Village in 2006. It's a showcase for their line of retro-modern hand-printed cards, stationery, and invitations, exclusive to this store. They also sell a selection of specially-chosen paper goods from other artists and designers. In a modern world dominated by email and computers, this is an oasis for those who treasure the art of print.

Beth und Amy Salvini stammen aus einer Familie, die seit drei Generationen im Druckergeschäft ist. 2006 eröffneten die Schwestern ihren winzigen Laden in der Christopher Street im West Village, der sich als wunderbare Schatzkammer entpuppt. Hier findet man von den Schwestern selbst entworfene, retro-moderne, handgedruckte Gruß- und Einladungskarten und exklusive Briefpapiere. Zudem verkaufen sie ausgewählte Papiere und Schreibwaren anderer Künstler und Designer. In der Zeit von E-Mail und Computer ist der Laden für die Liebhaber der Druckkunst eine wahre Oase.

Dans la famille Salvini, on est imprimeur depuis trois générations. Les deux sœurs Beth et Amy ont ouvert cette minuscule boutique sur Christopher Street en 2006 pour y présenter leurs cartes, papiers à lettre et cartons d'invitation rétro/modernes imprimés à la main et qu'on ne trouve qu'ici. Elles vendent aussi des articles en papier de designers et d'artistes triés sur le volet. Dans un monde moderne dominé par l'informatique et les courriels, c'est une oasis pour les amoureux de l'art de la papeterie.

Interior: Owners Amy Salvini-Swanson and Beth Salvini designed the cheery, light modern space.
Open: Mon 1pm–6pm (closed on Mon in summer); Tue–Fri 11am–7pm; Sat–Sun midday–6pm.
X-Factor: You can order custom invitations and cards printed on the shop's antique letterpress.

Interieur: Die freundliche, helle Innenausstattung wurde von den Besitzerinnen Amy Salvini-Swanson und Beth Salvini selbst entworfen.
Öffnungszeiten: Mo 13–18 Uhr (im Sommer montags geschlossen); Di–Fr 11–19 Uhr; Sa–So 12–18 Uhr.
X-Faktor: Man kann sich auf der antiken Druckerpresse persönliche Einladungen und Karten drucken lassen.

Intérieur : Amy Salvini-Swanson et Beth Salvini ont conçu cette espace gai, lumineux et moderne.
Horaires d'ouverture : Lun 13h–18h (fermé le lundi pendant l'été) ; Mar–Ven 11h–19h ; Sam–Dim midi–18h.
Le « petit plus » : Vous pouvez commander des cartons d'invitation et des cartes sur-mesure imprimés sur l'ancienne presse de la boutique.

Strand Book Store

828 Broadway, New York, NY 10003
☎ +1 212 473 1452
www.strandbooks.com

Subway: 14th Street-Union Square (L, N, Q, R, W, 4, 5, 6)

Manhattan's largest independent bookstore is the only one of 48 booksellers still in business from Union Square's "Book Row" era. Founded in 1927, the shop has 35,000 square feet of books. Browse new or out-of-print hardcovers, or pick through piles of secondhand paperbacks, art and photography books – nearly everything is sold at discount. There's something for every budget, from the one-dollar paperbacks sold on the sidewalk outside, to the 45,000-dollar copy of Ulysses, signed by James Joyce and Henri Matisse.

Manhattans größter unabhängiger Buchladen ist der letzte von ehemals 48 Buchhändlern aus der "Book Row"-Ära am Union Square. 1927 eröffnet, bietet er Bücher auf 3.250 Quadratmetern: neue und vergriffene Titel, Secondhand-Taschenbücher, Kunst- und Fotobände … und fast alles mit Preisnachlass. Und es findet sich etwas für jeden Geldbeutel, vom Taschenbuch aus der Grabbelkiste für 1 Dollar bis zur von James Joyce und Henri Matisse signierten Ulysses-Ausgabe für 45.000 Dollar.

Avec ses 3250 mètres carrés, Strand, fondée en 1927, est la plus grande librairie indépendante de Manhattan et la dernière des 48 qui bordaient autrefois le trottoir d'Union Square à Astor Place. Flânez entre les nouveautés et les éditions épuisées, farfouillez parmi les piles de romans, de livres d'art ou de photographie d'occasion, pratiquement tout est à prix réduit. Il y en a pour toutes les bourses, des livres de poche à 1 dollar vendus sur les étals à l'extérieur à l'exemplaire d'Ulysse signé par James Joyce et Henri Matisse proposé à 45 000 dollars.

Interior: Four floors of dusty steel shelves and books, books, books.
Open: Mon–Sat 9:30am–10:30pm; Sun 11am–10:30pm.
X-Factor: The Strand will also buy your used and unwanted books.

Interieur: Vier Etagen staubiger Metallregale voller Bücher, Bücher und nochmals Bücher.
Öffnungszeiten: Mo–Sa 9.30–22.30 Uhr; So 11–22.30 Uhr.
X-Faktor: The Strand kauft auch Ihre alten oder ungeliebten Bücher auf.

Intérieur : Quatre étages de rayonnages métalliques poussiéreux croulant sous des livres, encore des livres, toujours des livres.
Horaires d'ouverture : Lun–Sam 9h30–22h30 ; Dim 11h–22h30.
Le « petit plus » : The Strand rachète aussi vos livres d'occasion.

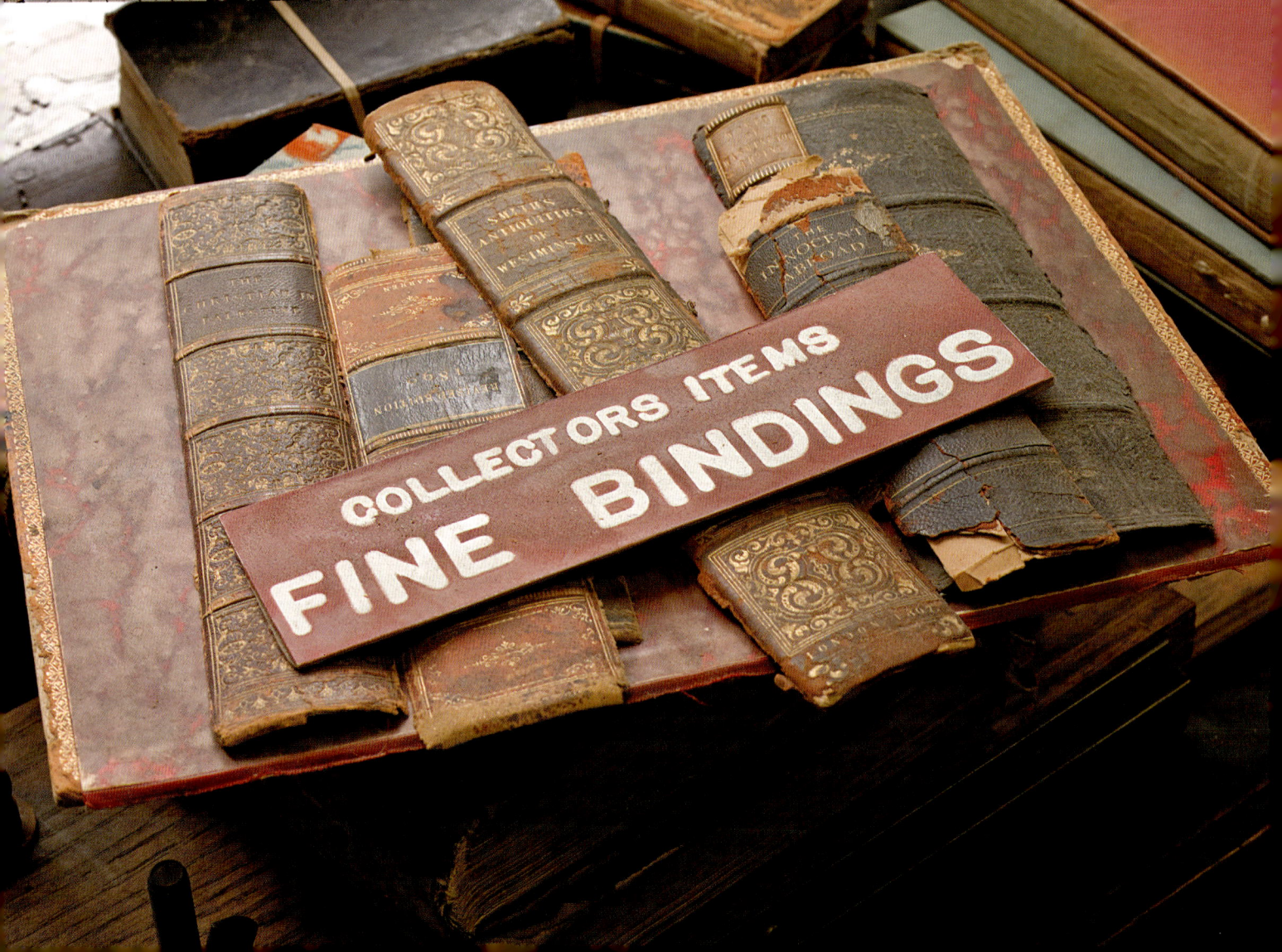

COLLECTORS ITEMS
FINE BINDINGS

POETRY

MYTHOLOGY POETRY

MYTHOLOGY POETRY

KING

...kstore is
...onic Detection

...fting is a crime.

BOOKS GO
BACK WHERE
YOU FOUND
THEM

Diane von Furstenberg

874 Washington Street, New York, NY 10014
☎ +1 646 486 4800
www.dvf.com
Subway: 14th Street (A, C, E), 8th Avenue (L)

This glittering jewel box of a store, opened in 2007, is such an extraordinary space that you may forget that you've come for shopping! Long before Diane von Furstenberg invented her iconic wrap dress, she was a passionate supporter and lover of fine arts. It's all on display in this retail space, with its lilac floor, and 77-step spiral staircase embedded with 3,000 Swarovski crystals. The works here from her private collection include pieces by Francesco Clemente, Robert Longo, Andreas Gursky, Damien Hirst, and of course the famous 1970s portrait of Diane herself by Andy Warhol.

Dieses 2007 eröffnete glitzernde Schmuckkästchen lässt manche Kundin glatt vergessen, dass sie eigentlich zum Shoppen vorbeigekommen ist! Lange bevor Diane von Furstenberg ihr ikonisches Wickelkleid konzipierte, war sie bereits eine leidenschaftliche Kunstsammlerin – was in diesem Shop mit seinem fliederfarbenen Boden und einer 77 Stufen umfassenden Wendeltreppe mit 3.000 Swarovski-Kristallen deutlich zum Ausdruck kommt. Die hier ausgestellten Werke aus der Privatsammlung der Designerin stammen von Künstlern wie Francesco Clemente, Robert Longo, Andreas Gursky und Damien Hirst – nicht zu vergessen das berühmte Porträt, das Andy Warhol in den 1970er Jahren von Diane selbst anfertigte.

Cet étincelant écrin, ouvert en 2007, est un lieu si extraordinaire qu'on en oublie qu'on est venu faire son shopping! Longtemps avant d'inventer sa fameuse robe wrap, Diane von Furstenberg était une grande mécène et amoureuse des arts, ce qu'attestent le sol lilas, l'escalier en spirale de 77 marches incrustées de 3000 cristaux Swarovski et les pièces provenant de sa collection privée qui incluent des œuvres de Francesco Clemente, Robert Longo, Andreas Gursky, Damien Hirst et, naturellement, son célèbre portrait réalisé par Andy Warhol dans les années 1970.

Interior: Award winning renovation of a landmark early-20th-century meat-packing building by Amale Andraos and Dan Wood of Workac.
Open: Mon–Wed, Fri–Sat 11am–7pm; Thu 11am–8pm; Sun midday–6pm.
X-Factor: The building is totally "green" with a green roof designed by French landscape architect Louis Benech, and a unique geothermal heating and cooling system that uses well water in place of fossil fuels.

Interieur: Preisgekrönte Sanierung eines Gebäudes vom Anfang des 20. Jahrhunderts im Meatpacking District (Design: Amale Andraos und Dan Wood von Workac).
Öffnungszeiten: Mo–Mi, Fr–Sa 11–19 Uhr; Do 11–20 Uhr; So 12–18 Uhr.
X-Faktor: Das Gebäude ist durch und durch „ökologisch" – mit einem begrünten Dach des französischen Landschaftsarchitekten Louis Benech sowie einem einzigartigen Erdwärmeheiz- und Kühlsystem.

Intérieur : Ancien abattoir du début du 20ᵉ siècle dont la restauration par Amale Andraos et Dan Wood, de Workac, a été primée.
Horaires d'ouverture : Lun–Mer, Ven–Sam 11h–19h ; Jeu 11h–20h ; Dim 12h–18h.
Le « petit plus » : Le bâtiment entièrement écologique possède une terrasse sur le toit aménagée par le paysagiste français Louis Benech et un système unique de chauffage et de climatisation à base d'eau de puits plutôt que de combustibles fossiles.

Jeffrey New York

449 West 14th Street, New York, NY 10014
☎ +1 212 206 1272
www.jeffreynewyork.com
Subway: 14th Street (A, C, E), 8th Avenue (L)

Yes, there are other stores in New York that carry designer goodies from Chanel, Céline, Lanvin, Prada, Saint Laurent, and Dior – but they aren't as fun as Jeffrey. This was one of the first retail outposts to open in Chelsea's art district in 1998. Relaxed and comfortable, Jeffrey's open spaces encourage comfortable browsing, and the house DJ plays a cool mix. Owner Jeffrey Kalinsky started his fashion career in shoes, so his selection is tremendous, the displays delicious – the Choos, Louboutins and Blahniks are tempting as candy.

Natürlich gibt es auch andere Läden in New York, die Chanel, Céline, Lanvin, Prada, Saint Laurent und Dio führen, aber da macht Einkaufen nicht so viel Spaß wie bei Jeffrey, das 1998 als eines der ersten kleineren Geschäfte in Chelseas Künstler- und Galerienviertel seine Pforten öffnete. Die offenen Flächen laden zum ausgiebigen Stöbern ein, wozu der hauseigene DJ einen coolen Mix auflegt. Besitzer Jeffrey Kalinsky begann seine Modekarriere mit Schuhen, daher ist seine Auswahl hier riesig und die Präsentation schlichtweg verführerisch – seine Choos, Louboutins und Blahniks sind einfach unwiderstehlich.

Certes, il y a d'autres boutiques à New York qui vendent Chanel, Céline, Lanvin, Prada, Saint Laurent et Dior, mais aucune d'aussi sympathique que Jeffrey. Ce fut l'une des premières à ouvrir dans le quartier des galeries à Chelsea en 1998. Ses espaces ouverts et décontractés invitent à flâner devant les portants et le DJ maison sait mettre de l'ambiance. Jeffrey Kalinsky ayant commencé sa carrière dans la chaussure, sa sélection est fabuleuse : Choo, Louboutin ou Blahnik, comment résister ?

Interior: Modern, minimal space in the old Nabisco biscuit warehouse.
Open: Mon–Wed, Fri 10am–8pm (Thu till 9pm); Sat 10am–7pm; Sun 12:30pm–6pm.
X-Factor: The friendly, fashion-savvy personal service; each salesperson trains at a regular Saturday morning "style clinic."

Interieur: Moderne, minimalistische Innenausstattung der ehemaligen Nabisco-Keksfabrik.
Öffnungszeiten: Mo–Mi, Fr 10–20 Uhr (Do bis 21 Uhr); Sa 10–19 Uhr; So 12.30–18 Uhr.
X-Faktor: Das freundliche und modekundige Personal nimmt jeden Samstagvormittag an Fortbildungskursen, den „Style Clinics", teil.

Intérieur : Espace moderne minimaliste dans une ancienne biscuiterie Nabisco.
Horaires d'ouverture : Lun–Mer, Ven 10h–20h (Jeu jusqu'à 21h) ; Sam 10h–19h ; Dim 12h 30–18h.
Le « petit plus » : Le service personnalisé et chaleureux. Chaque vendeur est un expert ès mode et un styliste personnel.

Printed Matter

195 10th Avenue, New York, NY 10011
☎ +1 212 925 0325
www.printedmatter.org
Subway: 23rd Street (C, E)

Founded in 1976 by a group of avant-garde artists including Sol LeWitt and Lucy Lippard, Printed Matter is a bookstore, reading room and exhibition space specializing in "art for the page" – books and magazines produced by artists. Inside their storefront, in the midst of the Chelsea gallery district, you'll find the most extensive collection of art books, prints and ephemera in the city, including more than 15,000 titles by 5,000 artists, including John Baldessari, Larry Clark, Keith Haring, Jenny Holzer, Ed Ruscha and Andy Warhol. If you're searching for a rare publication, or a limited edition, this is the best place to start.

Die 1979 von einer Gruppe Avantgarde-Künstler, darunter Sol LeWitt und Lucy Lippard, gegründete Buchhandlung Printed Matter ist gleichzeitig auch Lesezimmer und Ausstellungsraum für „Art for the Page" – also für Bücher und Magazine, die von Künstlern gestaltet wurden. Mitten in Chelseas Galerienviertel findet sich hier die größte Sammlung von Kunstbüchern, Drucken und Sammlerstücken der Stadt, mit über 15.000 Titeln von 5.000 Künstlern wie John Baldessari, Larry Clark, Keith Haring, Jenny Holzer, Ed Ruscha und Andy Warhol. Wer nach einem seltenen Buch oder einer limitierten Auflage sucht, ist hier genau richtig.

Fondé en 1976 au cœur du quartier des galeries à Chelsea par un groupe d'avant-gardistes dont Sol LeWitt et Lucy Lippard, Printed Matter est une librairie, un salon de lecture et une galerie consacrés à « l'art pour la page », à savoir aux livres et revues d'artistes. Vous y trouverez la collection de publications et de reproductions la plus complète, avec plus de 15000 titres par plus de 5000 artistes comme John Baldessari, Larry Clark, Keith Haring, Jenny Holzer, Ed Ruscha et Andy Warhol. Si vous cherchez un ouvrage rare ou une édition limitée, c'est ici qu'il faut commencer.

Interior: The shop is in the ground floor of a tenement apartment building, and was designed by architect Mark Jan Krayenhoff van de Leur.
Open: Mon–Wed 11am–7pm; Thu–Fri 11am–8pm; Sat 11am–7pm; Sun closed
X-Factor: The store's reading room is a gathering place for artists, curators and collectors young and old – a great place to linger and browse.

Interieur: Der Buchladen liegt im Erdgeschoss eines Wohnhauses und wurde vom Architekten Mark Jan Krayenhoff van de Leur entworfen.
Öffnungszeiten: Mo–Mi 11–19 Uhr, Do/Fr 11–20 Uhr, Sa 11–19 Uhr, So geschlossen
X-Faktor: Das Lesezimmer der Buchhandlung ist ein Treffpunkt für Künstler, Kuratoren und junge wie ältere Sammler – ein großartiger Ort zum Stöbern und Verweilen.

Intérieur : La boutique, conçue par l'architecte Mark Jan Krayenhoff van de Leur, se trouve au rez-de-chaussée d'un immeuble d'habitation.
Horaires d'ouverture : Lun–Mer 11h–19h ; Jeu–Ven 11h–20h ; Sam 11h–19h ; fermé le dimanche.
Le « petit plus » : Lieu de rendez-vous des artistes, conservateurs et collectionneurs de tous âges, le salon de lecture est un lieu passionnant où s'attarder.

R & Company

82 Franklin Street, New York, NY 10013
☎ +1 212 343 7979
www.r-and-company.com
Subway: Franklin Street (1), Canal Street (N, Q, R, W)

R & Company is a candy store for anyone who loves mid-century modern design. Co-owners Zesty Meyers and Evan Snyderman are passionate collectors and scholars who founded R in Brooklyn in 1997, then relocated to this 4,500-square-foot Tribeca space in 2000. They've amassed a treasure trove of tables, chairs, sofas, lighting and objects not only by iconic designers like Aalto, Castiglioni, Jacobsen and Mies van der Rohe, but also by lesser known figures like Swedish modernist Greta Magnusson Grossman. If there's something you want that's not on hand, they'll search for you; they also open their extensive library and collection to the public by appointment.

R & Company ist ein Paradies für Liebhaber modernen Designs aus der Mitte des 20. Jahrhunderts. Die beiden Eigentümer Zesty Meyers und Evan Snyderman sind leidenschaftliche Sammler und Kenner und gründeten R 1997 zunächst in Brooklyn, verlegten ihr Geschäft aber 2000 in dieses 420 Quadratmeter große Ladenlokal in Tribeca. Dort trugen sie eine wahre Fundgrube an Tischen, Stühlen, Sofas, Leuchten und Objekten von solchen Designikonen wie Aalto, Castiglioni, Jacobsen und Mies van der Rohe zusammen, aber auch von weniger bekannten Namen wie etwa der schwedische Designerin und Architektin Greta Magnusson Grossman. Auf Wunsch öffnen die Eigentümer ihre umfangreiche Bibliothek.

R & Company est un régal pour les amoureux du design des années 1950. Zesty Meyers et Evan Snyderman, collectionneurs et érudits passionnés, l'ont fondé à Brooklyn en 1997 avant dèmménager dans cet espace de 420 mètres carrés à Tribeca en 2000. Ils ont amassé un trésor de tables, de chaises, de canapés, de luminaires et d'objets de designers légendaires comme Aalto, Jacobsen et Mies van der Rohe mais aussi de créateurs moins connus comme la suédoise Greta Magnusson Grossman. Si l'objet de vos désirs n'y est pas, ils le rechercheront pour vous. Leur bibliothèque et leur collection sont également ouvertes au public sur rendez-vous.

Interior: Designed by Nick Dine and Mike Solis.
Open: Mon–Fri 11am–6pm; Sat midday–6pm.
X-Factor: Make sure to stop at the R Gallery, in the same location, which highlights the works of both vintage and contemporary designers like Finland's Ilmari Tapiovaara and Denmark's Verner Panton.

Interieur: Design von Nick Dine und Mike Solis.
Öffnungszeiten: Mo–Fr 11–18 Uhr; Sa 12–18 Uhr.
X-Faktor: Besuchen Sie unbedingt auch die R Gallery (im gleichen Gebäude), die Werke von klassischen und zeitgenössischen Designern wie den Finnen Ilmari Tapiovaara und den Dänen Verner Panton präsentiert.

Intérieur : Conçu par Nick Dine et Mike Solis.
Horaires d'ouverture : Lun–Ven 11h–18h ; Sam 12h–18h.
Le « petit plus » : Ne manquez pas de visiter la R Gallery, au même endroit, où sont exposés des designers d'hier et d'aujourd'hui comme le Finlandais Ilmari Tapiovaara ou le Danois Verner Panton.

Russ & Daughters

179 East Houston Street, New York, NY 10002
☎ +1 212 475 4880
www.russanddaughters.com
Subway: Lower East Side-2nd Avenue (F, V)

The delicacies brought to New York by the Eastern European Jews in the early 20th century – nova, bagels, bialys and smoked fish – are savored by New Yorkers of every ethnicity. For four generations, Russ & Daughters has been one of the most distinguished purveyors of caviar, breads and smoked fish. High quality (the bagels are hand-rolled), and a huge selection of unusual items like organic double smoked Danish salmon, have kept this evocative Lower East Side shop busy with customers for almost a century.

Die von osteuropäischen Juden zu Beginn des 20. Jahrhunderts nach New York gebrachten Delikatessen – Nova, Bagels, Bialys und Räucherfisch – sind bei allen New Yorkern beliebt. Seit vier Generationen ist Russ & Daughters einer der wichtigsten Lieferanten für Köstlichkeiten wie Kaviar, verschiedene Brotsorten und Räucherfisch-Spezialitäten. Hohe Qualität (handgemachte Bagels) und die große Auswahl ausgefallener Speisen, wie z. B. doppelt geräucherter dänischer Bio-Lachs, locken seit fast einem Jahrhundert Kunden in diesen nostalgischen Laden in der Lower East Side.

Les New-Yorkais, toutes origines confondues, raffolent des délices apportés par les Juifs d'Europe de l'Est au début du 20ᵉ siècle : nova, bagels, bialys et poissons fumés. Depuis quatre générations, Russ & Daughters est le plus éminent fournisseur en caviar, pains et poissons fumés. La grande qualité (les bagels sont roulés à la main) et une vaste sélection de produits rares comme le saumon danois bio fumé deux fois font que ce charmant traiteur ne désemplit pas depuis près d'un siècle.

Interior: Original, circa 1920s, New York deli, in a historic tenement building.
Open: Mon–Fri 8am–8pm; Sat 9am–7pm; Sun 8am– 5:30pm.
X-Factor: This is believed to be the first New York business to recognize "Daughters" in the name, rather than "Sons".

Interieur: Dieser Delikatessenladen in einem historischen Mietshaus hat noch seine Originalausstattung aus den 1920er-Jahren.
Öffnungszeiten: Mo-Fr 8–20 Uhr; Sa 9–19 Uhr; So 8–17.30 Uhr.
X-Faktor: Wahrscheinlich das erste New Yorker Geschäft, bei dem „Daughters" (Töchter) statt „Sons" (Söhne) als Namenszusatz verwendet wurde.

Intérieur : Décor des années 1920 d'origine, traiteur new-yorkais typique situé dans un immeuble d'habitation ancien.
Horaires d'ouverture : Lun–Ven 8h–20h ; Sam 9h–19h ; Dim 8h–17h30.
Le « petit plus » : Il semble que ce soit la première entreprise familiale à New York à avoir intégré les « filles » dans le nom, plutôt que l'habituel « & Sons ».

Freemans Sporting Club

8 Rivington Street, New York, NY 10002
☎ +1 212 673 3209
www.freemanssportingclub.com
Subway: Lower East Side-2nd Avenue (F, V), Bowery (J, M, Z)

Taavo Somer, the architect, and co-owner of Freemans restaurant, created this menswear shop around the corner from the restaurant. It shares the same woodsy, masculine design concept, heavy on the deer antlers, but instead of cocktails and food, the product is Somer's own line of rugged men's sportswear. F.S.C.'s camelhair jackets, pea coats, plaid wool shirts and herringbone tweed coats feel like they've been handed down to you by your grandfather, and the quality is tops – everything is handmade in America. You can have suits and jackets made to order – and, after your fitting is through, go next door and sit in one of Freemans's antique barber chairs for a professional straight-razor shave.

Taavo Somer, Architekt und Miteigner des um die Ecke gelegenen Restaurants Freemans, zeichnete auch für den Entwurf dieses Herrenausstatters verantwortlich. Hier herrscht das gleiche holzlastige, maskuline Designkonzept mit Hirschgeweihen, doch statt Cocktails und Speisen gibt es hier Somers eigene Kollektion robuster Sportswear. Die Kamelhaarjacketts, Kolanis, Flanellhemden und Tweedmäntel erinnern an Familienerbstücke und sind von bester Qualität – alles wird in Amerika handgefertigt. Außerdem bietet F.S.C. maßgeschneiderte Anzüge und Jacketts an, und nach der Anprobe kann man es sich nebenan in einem der antiken Friseursessel bequem machen und sich eine professionelle Messerrasur gönnen.

Taavo Somer, copropriétaire du Freemans, a ouvert cette boutique de mode masculine à deux pas de son restaurant. On y retrouve le même concept viril rustique (avec moult massacres) mais les cocktails et les plats ont cédé la place à la ligne de sportswear de Somer : vestes en poil de chameau, cabans, chemises écossaises en laine, manteaux en tweed, le tout semblant merveilleusement patiné par le temps. La qualité est irréprochable (tout est cousu main aux États-Unis). Vous pouvez commander vos costumes et vestes sur-mesure puis, après l'essayage, aller vous installer sur un des fauteuils de barbier pour un rasage au coupe-chou.

Interior: Hunting lodge and barbershop motif – old trunks, dark wood floors, antique barber chairs. Designed by architect/owner Taavo Somer.
Open: Mon–Fri 11am–8pm; Sat 11am–7pm; Sun midday–6pm.
X-Factor: The suits, made from vintage 1950s and 1960s wool, have a natural horsehair base, so they will look better over time and last a lifetime. They are hand tailored for F.S.C. by union shops in Brooklyn.

Interieur: Jagdlodge und Barbiersalon in einem, entworfen vom Architekten und Eigner Taavo Somer.
Öffnungszeiten: Mo–Fr 11–20 Uhr; Sa 11–19 Uhr; So 12–18 Uhr.
X-Faktor: Die Anzüge aus Wolle aus den 1950ern und 1960ern haben eine Rosshaareinlage – wodurch sie mit der Zeit immer besser aussehen und ein Leben lang halten – und werden in Brooklyner Schneidereien für F.S.C. handgeschneidert.

Intérieur : Atmosphère de pavillon de chasse et d'ancien barbier, conçu par l'architecte et propriétaire Taavo Somer.
Horaires d'ouverture : Lun–Ven 11h–20h ; Sam 11h–19h ; Dim 12h–18h.
Le « petit plus » : Les costumes, taillés dans des lainages vintage des années 1950 et 1960, ont une base en crin naturel qui les fait bien vieillir et durer toute une vie. Ils sont confectionnés à la main spécialement pour F.S.C. par des ateliers à Brooklyn.

Eileen's Cheesecake

17 Cleveland Place, New York, NY 10012
☎ +1 212 966 5585
www.eileenscheesecake.com
Subway: Spring Street (6)

In New York, the home of cheesecake, Eileen's is the favorite of food critics and fans alike. Eileen Avezzano opened this lower Manhattan shop on a quiet side street near Little Italy in 1976. Soon the crowds began to arrive, lured by her cakes which are perfect, neither too creamy nor too dry, light and not too sweet. Besides plain cheesecake, Eileen's offers 40 different flavors and fruit toppings, including chocolate, pumpkin, mocha, red velvet, and salted caramel. There's also a gluten-free and sugar-free cheesecake, in case you're feeling guilty.

In New York, der Heimat des Käsekuchens (New York Cheesecake), ist Eileen's bei Kuchenfans und Kritikern gleichermaßen beliebt. Eileen Avezzano eröffnete 1976 ihren Laden in einer ruhigen Seitenstraße von Lower Manhattan nahe Little Italy. Bald strömten die Kunden nur so herbei, angelockt von ihren perfekt cremigen, nicht zu trockenen, leichten und nicht zu süßen Kuchen. Neben dem klassischen Käsekuchen bietet Eileen's 40 verschiedene Sorten und Fruchtbeläge, darunter Schokolade, Kürbis, Mokka, "red velvet" und gesalzenes Karamel. Es gibt auch einen zuckerfreien Käsekuchen – für das gute Gewissen.

À New York, patrie du cheese-cake, ceux d'Eileen Avezzano font l'unanimité parmi les critiques et les fans. Depuis qu'elle a ouvert sa pâtisserie dans une petite rue tranquille près de Little Italy en 1976, on se bouscule pour acheter ses gâteaux parfaits : légers, ni trop crémeux, ni trop secs, ni trop sucrés. Outre les cheese-cakes nature, elle propose 40 parfums et coulis différents, dont chocolat, potiron, moka, fraise ou banane. Il y a également une version sans sucre, au cas où vous vous sentiriez coupable.

Interior: Tiny bakery with glass display case; walls hung with old pictures including a painting of the shop by artist Red Grooms.
Open: Mon–Fri 8am–9pm; Sat–Sun 10am–7pm.
X-Factor: The best-selling mini-cheesecakes, small enough for one person.

Interieur: Winzige Bäckerei mit Glasvitrine; an den Wänden alte Bilder, darunter auch ein Gemälde des Ladens von Red Grooms.
Öffnungszeiten: Mo–Fr 8–21 Uhr; Sa–So 10–19 Uhr.
X-Faktor: Die Mini-Käsekuchen, genau richtig für eine Person.

Intérieur : Minuscule pâtisserie avec des vitrines de gâteaux. Les murs sont tapissés de photos, parmi les lesquelles trône une peinture de la boutique signée Red Grooms.
Horaires d'ouverture : Lun–Ven 8h–21h; Sam–Dim 10h–19h.
Le « petit plus » : Les excellents mini cheese-cakes pour une personne.

Kiehl's

---

109 3rd Avenue, New York, NY 10003
☎ +1 212 677 3171
www.kiehls.com

Subway: 3rd Avenue (L),
14th Street-Union Square (N, Q, R, W, 4, 5, 6)

This is the flagship store of the well-known cosmetics, bath and skin-care brand. It's been on this block of 3rd Avenue since 1851. Kiehl's started out as an herbal apothecary, and there's a distinctly pharmaceutical and no-nonsense atmosphere here – the products, mostly herbal and organic, come in simple plastic bottles and tubes with plain labels. Kiehl's fragrance-free moisturizers and the shower gels, which come in more than a dozen scents, are hugely popular (Kiehl's has a 28-day Healthy Skin Guarantee, and skincare consultations are complimentary.).

Das Stammhaus der bekannten Kosmetik- und Hautpflegemarke existiert in diesem Häuserblock an der 3rd Avenue bereits seit 1851. Kiehl's war zunächst Kräuterapotheke, und diese nüchtern-medizinische Atmosphäre dominiert bis heute: Die Produkte, zumeist Naturprodukte aus biologischem Anbau, sind in einfache Kunststoffflaschen verpackt und tragen neutral gestaltete Etiketten, die auch optisch eine Zierde in jedem Badezimmer sind. Kiehl's parfümfreie Feuchtigkeitscremes und Duschgels in über einem Dutzend natürlicher Duftnoten erfreuen sich größter Beliebtheit. Immer und für jeden ein schönes Mitbringsel (Kiehl's hat eine 28-Tage-Garantie für gesunde Hautpflege, und die Beratung ist gratis.)

Cette boutique phare de la célèbre marque de produits de soins et de bain existe depuis 1851. À l'origine, c'était un apothicaire herboriste, d'où le côté sérieux et pharmaceutique de la ligne : principalement à base d'herbes et bios, les produits sont présentés dans des flacons en plastique et des tubes simples aux étiquettes sobres. On s'arrache ses crèmes hydratantes sans parfum et ses gels douche déclinés en plus de douze senteurs (Kiehl's offre une garantie de peau saine de 28 jours et les consultations dermatologiques sont gratuites).

Interior: Historic apothecary building, still contains some original counters and fixtures, filled with memorabilia including exhibits of the company's motorcycle collection.
Open: Mon–Sat 10 am–8 pm; Sun 11am–6 pm.
X-Factor: Kiehl's serious commitment to the environment. All packaging is recyclable, the labels use soy ink, and the store encourages customers to bring back their old bottles for reuse.

Interieur: Historische Apothekenausstattung mit teils erhaltenen Originaltheken und -schränken, angefüllt mit Andenken an die Motorradsammlung der Firma.
Öffnungszeiten: Mo–Sa 10–20 Uhr; So 11–18 Uhr.
X-Faktor: Kiehl's engagiert sich ernsthaft für die Umwelt. So sind alle Verpackungen recycelbar, für die Etiketten wird Sojatinte verwendet, und die Kunden können ihre alten Flaschen neu befüllen lassen.

Intérieur : Boutique d'apothicaire plus que centenaire qui contient encore du mobilier d'origine. Elle est remplie des pièces de la collection de motos de la compagnie.
Horaires d'ouverture : Lun–Sam 10h–20h ; Dim 11h–18h.
Le « petit plus » : Kiehl's s'est engagé pour la protection de l'environnement. Tous les emballages sont recyclables et la boutique encourage ses clients à rapporter leurs flacons vides pour les recharger.

Oak

28 Bond Street, New York, NY 10012
☎ +1212 677 12 93
www.oaknyc.com

Subway: Bleecker Street

At first glance the product range seems fairly ordinary to a European eye, but the Belgian and Scandinavian-influenced designers are of course freaky and hip to the domestic New York market. Clothing articles have to be close-fitting, black and deconstructed to be included in the Oak buyers' selection. The interior design of the store between Bowery and Broadway takes care of the rest. For instance, the payment counter (black, of course) is built in such a way that the person serving behind it is almost invisible. And the basement is like the Darkroom in Berghain, a club in Berlin. Great fun, in other words!

Auf Europäer wirkt das Sortiment zunächst nicht ungewöhnlich, unter Amerikanern gelten die belgisch und skandinavisch beeinflussten Designer freilich als freaky und hip. Vornehmlich eng, schwarz und dekonstruiert müssen die Kleidungsstücke geschnitten sein, um von den Oak-Kuratoren ausgewählt zu werden. Die Einrichtung des Ladengeschäfts zwischen Bowery und Broadway erledigt den Rest. Der (natürlich schwarze) Bezahltresen beispielsweise ist so konstruiert, dass von der dahinter agierenden Person kaum etwas zu sehen ist. Im Untergeschoss fühlt man sich an den Darkroom der Berliner Diskothek Berghain erinnert. Mit einem Wort: ein Riesenspaß!

Pour les Européens, l'assortiment n'a rien d'inhabituel, mais aux yeux des Américains, les designers d'influence belge et scandinave paraissent certainement bizarres et branchés. Pour être sélectionnés par les conservateurs d'Oak, les vêtements doivent être avant tout étroits, noirs et déconstruits. Le mobilier de la boutique entre Bowery et Broadway fait le reste. Le comptoir (noir, bien sûr) par exemple est conçu pour ne laisser presque rien voir de la personne qui se trouve derrière. Le sous-sol rappelle la darkroom de la discothèque berlinoise Berghain. En un mot : le pied !

Interior: The purist design of the sales areas is in keeping with the fashion on display. The predominant features are bright cement floors and black lacquered fixtures. Watch out for the steps leading down to the basement!
Open: Mon–Sat 11am–9pm, Sun 11am–8pm.
X-Factor: Their own-brand Oak collection has some pretty T-shirts on offer.

Interieur: Die Verkaufsräume sind der angebotenen Mode entsprechend puristisch gehalten. Heller Zementboden und schwarz lackierte Einbauten dominieren. Vorsicht auf den Treppenstufen ins Untergeschoß!
Öffnungszeiten: Mo–Sa 11–21 Uhr, So 11–20 Uhr.
X-Faktor: Die eigene Kollektion des Hauses hat hübsche T-Shirts zu bieten.

Intérieur : Les espaces réservés à la vente s'harmonisent avec la mode puriste qu'on y propose. Le sol en ciment clair et les installations fixes en laque noir dominent le reste. Attention aux marches du sous-sol !
Horaires d'ouverture : Lun-Sam 11 h–21 h ; Dim 11 h–20 h.
Le « petit plus » : La collection maison propose de jolis T-shirts.

Tiffany & Co.

727 5th Avenue, New York, NY 10022
☎ +1 212 755 8000
www.tiffany.com

Subway: 5th Avenue-53rd Street (E, V), 57th Street (F),
5th Avenue/59th Street (N, R, W)

Whose heart doesn't begin to beat a little faster when handed the famous Tiffany Blue box? As you enter the flagship store of this iconic American jeweler and silversmith, you may imagine yourself as Audrey Hepburn in Breakfast at Tiffany's, the movie version of Truman Capote's story. Founded in 1837 by Charles Lewis Tiffany, Tiffany sells timeless classics from every period of its distinguished history, from sparkling diamond engagement rings in the trademark Tiffany Setting, to sterling tableware, to Jean Schlumberger's lavish 1950s jewelry, and more recent exclusive creations by Elsa Peretti and Paloma Picasso.

Wessen Herz schlägt nicht höher beim Anblick einer der berühmten Schachteln in „Tiffany-Blau"? Beim Betreten des Stammhauses des berühmten amerikanischen Juweliers denkt so mancher an Audrey Hepburn in Frühstück bei Tiffany, der weltbekannten Filmversion von Truman Capotes Roman. Das 1837 von Charles Lewis Tiffany gegründete Unternehmen verkauft zeitlose Klassiker aus allen Epochen seiner einzigartigen Geschichte, von glänzenden Diamant-Verlobungsringen mit der geschützten Tiffany-Fassung über Tafelgeschirr aus Sterlingsilber bis hin zu Jean Schlumbergers prunkvollen Schmuckstücken aus den 1950er-Jahren und exklusiven Kreationen von Elsa Peretti und Paloma Picasso

Qui ne sentirait pas son cœur battre un peu plus fort en se voyant offrir une des fameuses boîtes « bleu Tiffany » ? En pénétrant dans la boutique phare du célèbre joaillier et orfèvre américain, on se prend pour Audrey Hepburn dans Diamants sur canapé, film adapté du roman de Truman Capote. Fondée en 1837 par Charles Lewis Tiffany, la maison propose d'intemporels classiques datant de toutes les époques de son histoire, des bagues de fiançailles en diamant à la monture caractéristique, à l'argenterie, aux somptueux bijoux des années 1950 de Jean Schlumberger et aux créations plus récentes d'Elsa Peretti et Paloma Picasso.

Interior: The building dates from 1940, and features a 9-foot-high figure of Atlas shouldering a large sculpted clock, which has adorned many Tiffany stores since 1853.
Open: Mon–Sat 10am–7pm; Sun midday–6pm.
X-Factor: There's something here for every budget, and the iconic Tiffany Blue box – introduced in 1878! – adds cachet and charm to even a modest gift.

Interieur: Genau wie die viele andere Tiffany-Läden seit 1853 ziert auch dieses Gebäude von 1940 eine 2,70 Meter große Atlas-Figur mit einer Uhr auf den Schultern.
Öffnungszeiten: Mo–Sa 10–19 Uhr; So 12–18 Uhr.
X-Faktor: Hier findet man etwas für jeden Geldbeutel – natürlich immer in der berühmten "Tiffany Blue"-Box (schon seit 1878!), die auch einem bescheideneren Geschenk Stil und Charme verleiht.

Intérieur : La façade de l'immeuble des années 1940 est ornée d'un atlante de 2,70 mètres de haut soutenant une horloge, emblème de nombreuses boutiques Tiffany depuis 1853.
Horaires d'ouverture : Lun–Sam 10h–19h ; Dim 12h–18h.
Le « petit plus » : Il y en a pour toutes les bourses et la célèbre boîte bleue de Tiffany (qui existe depuis 1878 !) ajoute du cachet au présent même le plus humble.

TIFFANY & CO

Bergdorf Goodman

754 5th Avenue, New York, NY 10019
☏ +1 212 753 7300
www.bergdorfgoodman.com
Subway: 5th Avenue/59th Street (N, R, W), 57th Street (F)

For nearly a century, Bergdorf Goodman has reigned as New York City's great department store. Opened at its current location in 1928 by Edwin Goodman, the store continues to set the standard for elegant high fashion and design. The mansard-roof building was designed to resemble the mansion that a typical client might have lived in. Its original French Renaissance styling of the interiors had no display racks; instead, personal shoppers brought selected items out to customers, one by one. Today, Bergdorf Goodman's eight floors hold the best of everything in the fashion world, from the classics like Oscar de la Renta and Valentino, to newcomers like Jason Wu.

Seit knapp einem Jahrhundert steht Bergdorf Goodman an der Spitze der großen New Yorker Kaufhäuser, und das an der derzeitigen Adresse 1928 von Edwin Goodman eröffnete Geschäft setzt auch weiterhin Standards im Bereich Eleganz, Mode und Design. Sein ursprünglich im französischen Renaissancestil gehaltenes Interieur besaß weder Regale noch Ausstellungsvitrinen, stattdessen brachten Einkaufsberater ausgewählte Waren zum Kunden. Heute bietet das Bergdorf Goodman auf acht Etagen das Beste der gesamten Modewelt – von klassischen Designern wie Oscar de la Renta und Valentino bis hin zu Newcomern wie Jason Wu.

Voici près d'un siècle que le roi des grands magasins dicte les normes en matière d'élégance en mode et design. Inauguré en 1928 par Edwin Goodman, ce bâtiment en marbre blanc anglais, initialement décoré dans le style de la Renaissance française, fut conçu pour ressembler à l'hôtel particulier d'un acheteur type. Il n'y avait pas de rayons : des assistants présentaient les articles aux clients pièce par pièce. Aujourd'hui, les neuf étages de Bergdorf Goodman proposent le meilleur de la mode : des classiques tels qu'Oscar de la Renta ou Valentino aux nouveaux venus comme Jason Wu.

Interior: The Paris-inspired mansard roof building on the former site of the Cornelius Vanderbilt II mansion was designed by architects Buchman & Kahn in 1928.
Open: Mon–Sat 10am–8pm; Sun 11am–6pm.
X-Factor: The store displays spectacular windows, especially during the holiday season.

Interieur: Die Architekten Buchman & Kahn entwarfen 1928 das von Pariser Bauwerken inspirierte Mansardengebäude auf dem ehemaligen Gelände der Villa von Cornelius Vanderbilt II.
Öffnungszeiten: Mo–Sa 10–20 Uhr, So 11–18 Uhr.
X-Faktor: Vor allem in der Weihnachtszeit präsentiert das Kaufhaus aufsehenerregende Schaufensterdekorationen.

Intérieur : Le bâtiment mansardé d'inspiration parisienne fut construit en 1928 par les architectes Buchman & Kahn sur l'emplacement de l'ancien hôtel particulier de Cornelius Vanderbilt II.
Horaires d'ouverture : Lun–Sam 10h–20h; Dim 11h–18h.
Le « petit plus » : Les vitrines du magasin sont spectaculaires, notamment pendant la période de Noël.

Apple Store

767 5th Avenue, New York, NY 10153
☎ +1 212 336 1440
www.apple.com

Subway: 5th Avenue/59th Street (N, R, W)

Approaching the Apple Store on 5th Avenue, you may feel like you're walking into a science-fiction movie. Opened in 2007, the store is underground – you enter at street level through a dramatic 32-foot structural glass cube with a glowing Apple logo floating above. The cube houses a transparent glass elevator wrapped in a crystalline circular glass staircase: whether you ride or walk down, it's a real trip. The futuristic entryway won architects Bohlin Cywinski Jackson a New York AIA award. BCJ also designed the spacious subterranean retail floor, with its clean lines, simple wooden furniture and Italian stone floors. It's hard to imagine a more perfect match of American architecture and product design: a visit to this store is like walking into your iPod.

Wer sich dem Apple Store an der 5th Avenue nähert, wähnt sich fast in einem Science-Fiction-Film: Der Eingang zum 2007 eröffneten, unterirdisch gelegenen Geschäft befindet sich ebenerdig in einem imposanten, zehn Meter hohen Glaskubus, in dem ein leuchtendes Apple-Logo schwebt. Von dort führt ein transparenter Glasfahrstuhl, umgeben von einer gläsernen Wendeltreppe, in das lichtdurchflutete Ladeninnere. Mit diesem futuristischen Eingangsbereich gewann das Architekturbüro Bohlin Cywinski Jackson 2007 den New York AIA Award. Eine perfektere Kombination amerikanischer Architektur und amerikanischen Produktdesigns kann man sich kaum vorstellen – ein Besuch dieses Apple Store ist wie ein Spaziergang durch den eigenen iPod.

En s'avançant vers le magasin Apple sur la 5th Avenue, on a l'impression d'entrer dans son iPod. Inauguré en 2007, il se trouve en sous-sol. On y accède par un cube en verre géant sur lequel flotte le célèbre logo. Il abrite un ascenseur vitré ceint d'un escalier circulaire transparent. Que vous montiez ou descendiez, l'effet est saisissant. Cette entrée futuriste a valu aux architectes Bohlin Cywinski Jackson d'être primés par le New York AIA. Ils ont également conçu les spacieux espaces de vente tout en lignes épurées, vitrines en acier et sols en dalles italiennes. Difficile d'imaginer un mariage plus parfait entre l'architecture américaine et le design de produit.

Interior: Located in the underground retail concourse of the white marble and black glass International style General Motors Building (built 1968). The first skyscraper ever built by architect Edward Durell Stone.
Open: 24 hours a day/365 days a year.
X-Factor: Head for the Genius Bar, where you can take a seat and have your troublesome iPods and MacBooks diagnosed by a specially-trained Apple tech person, not to mention the customer-friendly open hours.

Interieur: Der Store befindet sich im Untergeschoss des General Motors Building (erbaut 1968), dem von weißem Marmor und schwarzem Glas geprägten ersten Wolkenkratzer des Architekten Edward Durell Stone.
Öffnungszeiten: 24 Stunden täglich an 365 Tagen im Jahr.
X-Faktor: In der Genius Bar kann man in Ruhe Platz nehmen, während ein Apple-Techniker sich um den defekten iPod oder das MacBook kümmert – und das jederzeit (siehe Öffnungszeiten).

Intérieur : Situé au sous-sol du General Motors Building construit en 1968 dans le style International tout en marbre blanc et verre fumé. (Le premier gratte-ciel de l'architecte Edward Durell Stone.)
Horaires d'ouverture : 24h/24, 365 jours par an.
Le « petit plus » : Outre les horaires d'ouverture cités plus haut, le « Genius bar » où vous pouvez apporter votre iPod récalcitrant pour le faire diagnostiquer par un expert.

Barneys New York

660 Madison Avenue, New York, NY 10065
☎ +1 212 826 8900
www.barneys.com

Subway: 5th Avenue/59th Street (N, R, W)

Barneys New York is more than a store, it's a gallery of contemporary New York fashion. Founded as a men's discount retailer in 1923, it turned into an arbiter of high style in the 1970s, when it was located in Chelsea. Currently, its New York flagship location occupies a 240,000-square-foot building on Madison Avenue filled with the most intriguing selections from the world's top designers. At Barneys you'll find both big names and unknowns. They introduced Armani to the U.S., and he's still here, along with men's and women's clothing and accessories from Prada, Dries van Noten, Christian Louboutin, 3.1 Phillip Lim – and much more.

Barneys New York ist weniger ein Geschäft als eine Galerie für zeitgenössische New Yorker Mode. 1923 als preiswerter Herrenausstatter gegründet, entwickelte es sich in den 1970er-Jahren, damals noch in Chelsea beheimatet, zur Speerspitze gehobenen Stils. New Yorks Flagship-Store an der Madison Avenue bietet auf 22.300 Quadratmetern eine faszinierende Auswahl der weltbesten Designer. Doch Barneys präsentiert neben bekannten Namen auch (noch) unbekannte: So brachte das Haus die Marke Armani in die USA – die man hier noch immer findet, gemeinsam mit Herren- und Damenbekleidung von Prada, Dries van Noten, Christian Louboutin, 3.1 Phillip Lim und vielen anderen.

Barneys est plus qu'un magasin, c'est une galerie de la mode new-yorkaise contemporaine. Fondé en 1923 comme boutique de vêtements masculins au rabais, il s'est transformé en arbitre de l'élégance dans les années 1970 quand il se trouvait à Chelsea. Le flagship store de New York occupe aujourd'hui un immeuble de 22 300 mètres carrés sur Madison Avenue, rempli d'une sélection des meilleurs stylistes du monde. On y trouve les grands noms comme des inconnus. C'est ici qu'Armani s'est fait connaître aux États-Unis et il y est toujours, aux côtés de Prada, Dries van Noten, Christian Louboutin, 3.1 Phillip Lim et de bien d'autres.

Interior: Classic French limestone building, completed in 1993, designed by Peter Marino, who also did the modern residential-like interiors.
Open: Mon–Fri 10am–8pm; Sat 10am–7pm; Sun 11am–7pm.
X-Factor: In-the-know New Yorkers save their pennies for Barneys' famous Warehouse Sale in August, where prices are cut from 50 to 75%.

Interieur: Klassischer Kalksteinbau, 1993 nach einem Entwurf von Peter Marino fertiggestellt, der auch die moderne, wohnliche Inneneinrichtung gestaltete.
Öffnungszeiten: Mo–Fr 10–20 Uhr; Sa 10–19 Uhr; So 11–19 Uhr.
X-Faktor: New Yorker Einkaufsprofis sparen für Barneys berühmten Ausverkauf im August, wenn die Preise um 50 bis 75% reduziert werden.

Intérieur : Immeuble à la française en pierre calcaire, achevé en 1993. Conçu par Peter Marino qui a également réalisé les intérieurs sobres et modernes.
Horaires d'ouverture : Lun–Ven 10h–20h ; Sam 10h–19h ; Dim 11h–19h.
Le « petit plus » : Les New-Yorkais avisés mettent leurs sous de côté pour la célèbre grande braderie de Barneys en août, avec des rabais de 50 à 75%.

J.Crew

1035 Madison Ave, New York, NY 10075
☎ +1 212 249 3869

Subway: 77 and 86 St.

Of all J.Crew branches now in Manhattan, this one is the best, as it is the smallest and run with the greatest care and attention. The product range is always selected with supreme skill, reflecting the needs of an upmarket neighbourhood that stocks up here with basics which are top-quality, yet relatively inexpensive. You can also find evening wear and wedding outfits for the odd special event without breaking the bank. For other occasions the relaxed-fit, cashmere "boyfriend" V-neck sweaters are a perfect choice – you can never have enough of them.

Von allen J.Crew-Filialen in Manhattan ist diese die beste, weil kleinste und am aufmerksamsten geführte von immerhin insgesamt acht. Das Sortiment ist stets auf den Punkt zusammengestellt und reflektiert die Bedürfnisse einer eleganten Nachbarschaft, die sich hier mit hochwertigen, dabei im Vergleich günstigen Basics eindeckt. Aber auch Abendkleider und Brautmode für spontane Anlässe sind hier nicht zu teuer zu finden. Zu anderen Gelegenheiten leisten die leger geschnittenen (Boyfriend)-Kaschmirpullover mit V-Ausschnitt perfekte Dienste. Man kann davon leider nicht genug haben.

Parmi toutes les filiales J.Crew de Manhattan, pas moins de huit, c'est la première parce que la plus petite et celle qui est tenue avec le plus de soin. La collection y est toujours composée de l'essentiel et reflète les besoins d'un voisinage élégant qui s'approvisionne ici en basiques haut de gamme mais relativement bon marché. On y trouve aussi des robes de soirée et de mariée pas trop chères pour les besoins imprévus. Et pour d'autres occasions, les pulls cachemire en V à la coupe décontractée (Boyfriend) rendent d'incomparables services. On n'en a jamais assez.

Interior: Designer items (Warren Platner, Serge Mouille) are placed sparingly but effectively, and white washed wooden floors create a stylish, feel-good factor.
Open: Mon–Sat 10am–9pm, Sunday 11am–6pm
X-Factor: Every J.Crew store has a red phone on the wall, connected to their "We'll find it for you" service – for items you have set your heart on, but which are not available in-store.

Interieur: Sparsam aber effektvoll eingesetzte Designerstücke (Warren Platner, Serge Mouille) und geschlämmte Holzböden sorgen für ein schickes Wohlgefühl.
Öffnungszeiten: Mo–Sa 10–21 Uhr, So 11–18 Uhr
X-Faktor: In jedem J.Crew-Laden hängt ein roter Telefonapparat, der mit dem „We'll find it for you"-Service verbindet. Für die Suche nach dem gewünschten und momentan nicht greifbaren Herzensstück.

Intérieur Les objets design (Warren Platner, Serge Mouille) et les sols en bois créent une impression d'élégance et de bien-être.
Horaires d'ouverture : Lun–Sam 10 h–21 h, Dim 11 h–18 h.
Le « petit plus » : Dans chaque boutique J.Crew, un téléphone est raccordé au service « We'll find it for you » qui recherche dans les filiales du pays le coup de cœur indisponible.

Index | Index | Index

Imprint | Impressum | Imprint

© 2014 TASCHEN GmbH
Hohenzollernring 53, D-50672 Köln
www.taschen.com

© 2014 VG Bild-Kunst, Bonn for the works of Harry Bertoia
and Ludwig Mies van der Rohe.

© 2009 for the works of Charles and Ray Eames:
Eames Office, Venice, CA, www.eamesoffice.com.

Compiled, Edited & Layout by
Angelika Taschen, Berlin

General Project Manager
Stephanie Paas, Cologne

Editorial Coordination
Nina Schumacher, Cologne

Illustrations
Olaf Hajek, www.olafhajek.com

Graphic Design & Maps
Eggers + Diaper, Berlin

Texts
Daisann McLane, New York
Angelika Taschen, Berlin

Text research
Emily Mottolese, New York

German Translation
Franca Fritz & Heinrich Koop, Straelen

French Translation
Philippe Safavi, Paris

Lithograph Manager
Thomas Grell, Cologne

Printed in China
ISBN 978-3-8365-5487-9

To stay informed about TASCHEN and our upcoming titles, please subscribe
to our free magazine at www.taschen.com/magazine, download our magazine app
for iPad, follow us on Twitter and Facebook, or e-mail your questions to
contact@taschen.com.